A BOOK ADDICT'S TREASURY

A BOOK ADDICT'S TREASURY

JULIE RUGG & LYNDA MURPHY

FRANCES LINCOLN LIMITED
PUBLISHERS

A BOOK ADDICT'S TREASURY

Frances Lincoln Limited
4 Torriano Mews
Torriano Avenue
London NW5 2RZ
www.franceslincoln.com

Introduction copyright © 2006 Julie Rugg & Lynda Murphy
For full acknowledgments, see page 226

First Frances Lincoln edition: 2006

ISBN 10: 0-7112-2685-7
ISBN 13: 978-0-7112-2685-2

Printed and bound in Singapore
by KHL Printing Co Pte Ltd

2 4 6 8 9 7 5 3

CONTENTS

For Lyra and Katie

INTRODUCTION:
A TALE OF TWO READERS

She shouldn't have been a reader, but she was. Julie's rogue gene had already shown itself in her Auntie Gladys: she was, by Auntie Lily's account, a bookish fishwife, conspicuous on the Hull docks. Their sister, Julie's mother, had been more readily seduced by the big screen, and Julie's first reading was confined to a random row of fifteen movie star albums her mother had kept from the 1950s, dealing with the likes of Alan Ladd and Ruth Roman in awe-struck prose ('Lucky June Allyson can gather her own oranges, so husband Dick Powell is never short of fruit'; 'Janet Blair's blouse is essentially simple in line. It's the handpainted fish and dragonflies which strike a unique fashion note'). Later, her mother found a taste for salacious bodice-rippers. Julie thought these altogether puzzling in places, but read them nonetheless.

Julie was an early reader, but became voraciously so when a square modern block of branch library opened on her council estate. Suddenly she had Nancy Drew and the Hardy Boys and the Three Investigators and – very quickly – John Wyndham and P. G. Wodehouse and J. J. Marrick too, whose books were an interminable series of police thrillers with covers that, in subtly different shades, all showed a foggy London. Her straying into the adult section was only once questioned, when she pushed over the counter a copy of Solzhenitsyn's *Cancer Ward*. They said she wouldn't understand it, but nevertheless she was allowed to take it. Julie tried everything. When she was old enough she got on the bus and went to the as yet unexhausted shelves of the Central Library, and after that went even further afield to raid other branch libraries. As the quotations indicate, librarians and libraries have become the subject of stock jokes but she – like Germaine Greer – enjoys a sense of peace and belonging when entering any library.

By the time she went to university in 1982 she had become well acquainted with the two readily accessible second-hand bookshops in town. One, tucked away in a covered arcade by the market, had an upstairs room full of tattered cast-offs that could be bought for pence. The other was a self-consciously alternative record shop carrying a wall of books that had been sold by departing students in black polo-necks: it was all Sartre and Hobsbawm, slim Penguin plays and black-backed classics. But 1986 was a key year. The summer was spent in London with *Driff's Guide to All the Second Hand Book Shops* and disposable income from working part-time in the British Museum café. By then it was Peregrine and Picador and innumerable Victorian novelists, the cheaper the better. By the late 1980s her then-boyfriend had developed a hugely lucrative ability to empty pub trivia machines, so funding extended book hunts in the second-hand and charity shops of Sheffield and Northampton. At the end of the day, the book bags were emptied out over a café tabletop, pages were riffled and bargains crowed over. These were times akin to Laski and Holmes' splendid days in Oxford.

People who say they don't have time to read simply don't want to. For a true reader – one of McMurtry's 'Giant Pandas' – a day of work reading doesn't slake the appetite for more amenable reading at home: in the minutes before bed and in the bath; whilst eating a slice of toast; on train journeys back from meetings. Pregnancy is the very best time to read, offering as it does an incontrovertible excuse for immobility. Julie read Pullman's *His Dark Materials* trilogy in the final weeks before her daughter was born, and remembers making her husband buy and bring home the second instalment in his lunch break because she couldn't wait until teatime. Having a child simply means that more of the books have pictures, and are read aloud.

Compiling this anthology has been the desultory work of decades. In her twenties Julie started to gather quotations that made her smile at her own sometimes excessive bookish behaviour. The decision to draw it all together and find a publisher was entirely impulsive. However, she realised that there wasn't enough material and that she needed more. She was most fortunate in being able to secure a partner for this enterprise.

Lynda can't honestly say that there were no books in the house when she was a child, but she simply can't remember seeing any. Being more of a buyer than a borrower, she organised her own library so that friends could borrow *her* books for a small fee, but never pursued these entrepreneurial beginnings. Her collection included *Jane Eyre* which, far from being a children's book, is nevertheless sometimes marketed as such to traumatise young girls. One of her earliest bookish moments was being horrified by the child Jane's discovery that Helen had died beside her in the night. She re-read that episode several times but always secretly, concerned that a similar fate would befall her if her morbid obsession was discovered. Her great-aunt had, from one of the book clubs, a full set of Dickens. This was proudly displayed on the bottom shelf of a glass-fronted cabinet. Flicking through their pages, Lynda became acquainted with the names of Pip, Uriah Heep, Miss Havisham, Bill Sykes and Mrs Skewton. She then managed to get through five years of university and well into adulthood without reading another word of Dickens.

Working in one of York's retail institutions – a well-known if not quite famous antiquarian bookshop – Lynda witnessed bibliomania at first hand. She saw collectors so obsessive that they would do almost anything to secure a purchase, even if the volume was never removed from its package once procured. She spent many cold hours in that bookshop, and was regularly ousted from the only warm spot – next to the fire – by someone so caught up in reading that he would not notice the backs of his trousers slowly scorching. For Orwell, similarly employed, 'the top of a book is the place where every bluebottle prefers to die.' After an eight-hour stint standing in the cold there were moments when Lynda would gladly have swapped places with the bluebottle, just in order to lie down. But there were few things more exciting than a large delivery of books from the treasured collection of someone who had recently joined the bluebottles on the top shelf. Handling first editions, beautifully designed dust wrappers hugging favourite stories, early Faber & Faber poetry collections and the simple but perfectly colour-coded Penguins made her only ever want to read and adorn her bookshelves with second-hand books. And she also met her husband there: he is one of those creatures who can spend an immobile three hours reading in a bookshop, then sigh, dart out of the shop and, Narnia-like, enter the real world again.

When Julie first mentioned that she was collecting quotations, Lynda was most willing to rack her brains for the merest hint of the possibility that a particular book might yield ready material. Arthur Ransome would have entirely disapproved of their speed-reading dozens of texts, chasing down half-remembered incidents. (Wasn't Daniel Deronda described standing outside a bookshop? That guy reading the story on the radio – was it Garrison Keillor?) They were at times astonishingly lucky in opening a book at exactly the place to find a pithy and eloquent passage that was just right. Fortune did not always smile on the endeavour: it took a full afternoon in a state of escalating exasperation to find the few lines tucked away in *Ravenshoe*. They ram-raided the commonly anthologised quotations, and rejected the ones that were pompous, the ones that were tired, and the ones that made them yawn. They were almost childishly rigorous in only including quotations located 'in situ': it became a big game hunt, and a few friends pitched in with their own contributions. On the way, their literary favourites included Leigh Hunt (tearfully sentimental about books), Arnold Bennett (enthusiastic but pragmatic) and Larry McMurtry (childishly excitable). There were a few enemies too: John Cowper Powys (impossibly fey), George Orwell (tending to grumpiness) and Ruskin (simply slappable). The final manuscript reached the publisher through the enthusiasm of David Solkin, who spied it over Lynda's shoulder.

It is possible to order quotations in lots of different ways. The duller anthologies look to chronology or, even duller, to the alphabetical listing of authors. The idea behind this selection is to draw together quotations and extracts that comment upon the same theme, and then build a structure of complementary and contradictory responses. These groups are then, sometimes a little arbitrarily, ranged under broader headings. An Index of Authors eases the task of chasing down favourites, and will help critics pinpoint the more risible omissions. A fuller index is provided, and for the people who like that kind of thing, it's exactly the kind of thing they'll like.

York 2005

I. 'FULL SAIL ON THE SEA OF DREAMS': ADVENTURES IN READING

There is no such subject on which the great manifest such duplicity as on this subject of their early reading. We are all familiar with the Great Poet who in childhood dragged the infolio Spenser from his grandfather's Library and sat small and immersed under and in the 'Faerie Queene'. This meandering and inconclusive poem is doubtless of great importance in the history of English prosody. There are moments, even, when those Spenserian stanzas elope with such consummate ease that they convey the impression of important poetry. Nor should I deny the charm of Spenser, an unhappy man, who, in that bleak tower of Kilkolman, struggled through dark days. Besides, he was a friend of Raleigh and Philip Sidney, and wrote some charming things on the subject of Chaucer. A desirable man, and not one whom I should wish to deride. I contend only that that long poem of his, with its reiterant melody, is not a poem which should appeal to any healthy child.

And yet – take any autobiography of any leading poet, and you will find the bit about the Spenser folio dragged along his childhood. It simply isn't true.

Harold Nicolson, 'How to read books' (1937).

At any moment the impulse might seize me; and then, if the book was in reach, I had only to walk the floor, turning the pages as I walked, to be swept off full sail on the sea of dreams. The fact that I could not read added to the completeness of the illusion, for from those mysterious blank pages I could evoke whatever my fancy chose. Parents and nurses, peeping at me through the cracks of doors . . . noticed that I often held the book upside down, but that I never failed to turn the pages, and that I turned them at about the right pace for a person reading aloud as passionately and precipitately as was my habit.

Edith Wharton, *A Backward Glance* (1934).

Before I could read, almost a baby, I imagined that God, this strange thing or person I heard about, was a book. Sometimes it was a large book standing upright and half open and I could see the print inside but it made no sense to me. Other times the book was smaller and inside were sharp flashing things. The smaller book was, I am sure now, my mother's needle-book, and the sharp flashing things were her needles with the sun on them.

I was so slow learning to read that my parents had become worried about me. Then suddenly, with a leap as it were, I could manage quite long words. Soon I could make sense of the fairy stories Irish Granny sent – the red, the blue, the green, the yellow. Then she sent *The Heroes, The Adventures of Ulysses, Perseus and Andromeda*. I read everything I could get hold of. There was the usual glassed-in bookcase at the end of the sitting-room, but it was never locked, the key was lost, and the only warning was that we must keep it shut, for the books must be protected against insects.

I can still see the volumes of the *Encyclopaedia Britannica* that I never touched, a large Bible and several history books, yellow-backed novels and on the top shelf a rather odd selection of poets, Milton, Byron, then Crabbe, Cowper, Mrs Hemans, also *Robinson Crusoe, Treasure Island, Gulliver's Travels, Pilgrim's Progress*.

My nurse, who was called Meta, didn't like me much anyway, and complete with a book it was too much. One day she found me crouched on the staircase reading a bowdlerised version of the Arabian Nights in very small print.

She said, 'If all you read so much, you know what will happen to you? Your eyes will drop out and they will look at you from the page.'

'If my eyes dropped out I wouldn't see,' I argued.

She said, 'They drop out except the little black points you see with.'

I half believed her and imagined my pupils like heads of black pins and all the rest gone. But I went on reading.

Jean Rhys, *Smile Please: An Unfinished Autobiography* (1981).

My dealings with literature go back, I suppose, some thirty and three years. We came together thus, literature and I. It was in a kitchen at midday, and I was waiting for my dinner, hungry and clean, in a tartan frock with a pinafore over it. I had washed my own face, and dried it, and I remember that my eyes smarted with lingering soap, and my skin was drawn by the evaporation of moisture on a cold day. I held in my hand a single leaf which had escaped from a printed book. How it came into that chubby fist I cannot recall. The reminiscence begins with it already there. I gazed hard at the paper, and pretended with all my powers to be completely absorbed in its contents; I pretended to ignore someone who was rattling saucepans at the kitchen range . . .

I could not read, I could not distinguish one letter from another. I only knew that the signs and wonders constituted print, and I played at reading with intense earnestness. I actually felt learned, serious, wise, and completely superior, something like George Meredith's 'Dr Middleton'. Would that I could identify this my very first literature! I review three or four hundred books annually now; out of crass, saccharine, sentimentality, I would give a year's harvest for the volume from which that leaf was torn, nay, for the leaf alone, as though it might be a Caxton. I remember that the paper was faintly bluish in tint, veined, and rather brittle. The book was probably printed in the eighteenth century. Perhaps it was Lavater's *Physiognomy* or Blair's *Sermons*, or Burnet's *Own Time*. One of these three, I fancy, it must surely have been.

Arnold Bennett, *The Truth about an Author* (1902).

To begin at the beginning then, the first book in the world from which I am conscious of receiving any sort of ecstasy was one entitled 'Lottie's Visit to Grandmamma'. From the early pages of it I was first taught to read and the beginnings were anything but ecstatic. Looking now at the volume, I perceive that the first page is divided off (I suppose by the careful hand of my governess) into two lines at a time, and I gather that two lines a day were as much as I could just then manage. I fancy also from marks upon the page that battles of blood and tears were fought over every word, and one word of three syllables is underlined with desperate emphasis as though here was an obstacle never to be surmounted. So I struggled, I daresay, for months and months, and then suddenly liberation came and I paced ahead. I can remember exactly the moment at which my first consciousness of ecstasy arrived. Lottie and her little friend had been permitted by their Grandmamma to go for a walk on the beach while a gale was blowing; there is a picture of them clutching their funny little straw hats, their short, spindle legs wabbling below them, and then suddenly an old gentleman's umbrella is blown away and Lottie and her little friend, being not modern children at all but always rather on the watch for succouring the aged and doing good to invalids, rush after and, in spite of a terrific battle with the gale, secure it for the old gentleman, who thanks them in the most courtly and early-Victorian manner. I can remember very vividly indeed that this dramatic passage was a revelation to me. I saw it all so sharply that there was no need for the charming picture. My own personal life was instantly doubled, no passages that I read afterwards, whether in the pages of Marryat, or Melville or of Conrad, gave me more vividly the impression of the perils of the sea than did these few lines; the windows were opened and I knew once and for all what Reading could do for one.

Hugh Walpole, *These Diversions: Reading* (1926).

It must, I think, have been in the Easter term of 1905 – that is, when I was nearly twelve – that both my misery and the neurosis that was associated with it reached their critical point. I had taken to reading with all the zest and fury with which one takes to it at that age. Books were my opium and I could hardly bear to have one out of my hand. Boys' adventure stories, especially when they led into remote regions of the world, were my first taste and from them I went on to melodramas written for adults. These sometimes affected me powerfully. During the holidays, a couple of years before, my mother had started to read me *Oliver Twist*, but had been obliged to put it down because it gave me nightmares. Now, lying full length on the divan in the library, I devoured *The Deemster* by Hall Caine. As I read it I imagined that my parents, by some unlucky stroke, had lost all their money, that we should presently sink into a frightening poverty and be obliged to seek lodgings in one of the more dismal quarters of a large town. I even imagined that my father had got into debt, or into some trouble that was worse than debt, and was on the point of being carried off to prison. So real did this imaginary catastrophe become to me that every day I scanned the red, purple-veined face of the headmaster in the expectation that he would call me to his study and tell me that he had just received – a letter. But he never sent for me, nothing happened, and gradually I recovered my equanimity.

Gerald Brenan, *A Life of One's Own* (1962).

I was made to read without explanation, under the usual fear of punishment. And on a day that I remember it came to me that 'reading' was not 'the Cat lay on the Mat', but a means to everything that would make me happy. So I read all that came within my reach. As soon as my pleasure in this was known, deprivation from reading was added to my punishments. I then read by stealth and the more earnestly.

Rudyard Kipling, Something of Myself (1937).

'I can always tell when you're reading somewhere in the house,' my mother used to say. 'There's a special silence, a *reading* silence.'

Francis Spufford, The Child that Books Built (2002).

*****

The old gentleman was a very respectable-looking personage, with a powdered head and gold spectacles. He was dressed in a bottle-green coat with a black velvet collar; wore white trousers; and carried a smart bamboo cane under his arm. He had taken up a book from the stall, and there he stood, reading away, as hard as if he were in his elbow-chair, in his own study. It is very possible that he fancied himself there, indeed; for it was plain, from his abstraction, that he saw not the book-stall, nor the street, nor the boys, nor, in short, anything but the book itself; which he was reading straight through: turning over the leaf when he got to the bottom of a page, beginning at the top line of the next one, and going regularly on, with the greatest interest and eagerness.

Charles Dickens, Oliver Twist (1837–9).

There is a class of street readers, whom I can never contemplate without affection – the poor gentry, who, not having wherewithal to buy or hire a book, filch a little learning at the open stalls – the owner, with his hard eye, casting envious looks at them all the while, and thinking when will they have done. Venturing tenderly, page after page, expecting every moment when he shall interpose his interdict, and yet unable to deny themselves the gratification, they 'snatch a fearful joy'. Martin B., in this way, by daily fragments, got through two volumes of *Clarissa*, when the stall-keeper damped his laudable ambition, by asking him (it was in his younger days) whether he meant to purchase the work. M. declares, that under no circumstances of his life did he ever peruse a book with half the satisfaction which he took in those uneasy snatches.

Charles Lamb, 'Detached thoughts on books and reading' (1833).

I'm thirty-two years old . . . which means I've been reading for twenty-six years. Twenty-six years since the furze of black marks between the covers of *The Hobbit* grew lucid, and released a dragon. Twenty-six years therefore since the primary discovery that the dragon remained internal to me. Inside my head, Smaug hurtled, lava gold, scaly green. And nothing showed. Wars, jokes, torrents of faces would fill me from other books, as I read on, and none of that would show either. It made a kind of intangible shoplifting possible, I realised when I was eleven or so. If your memory was OK you could descend on a bookshop – a big enough one so that the staff wouldn't hassle a browser – and steal the contents of books by reading them. I drank down *1984* while loitering in the O section of the giant Heffers store in Cambridge. When I was full I carried the slopping vessel of my attention carefully out of the shop. Nobody at the cash desks could tell that I now contained Winston Smith's telescreen chanting its victories, O'Brien's voice admitting that the Thought Police got him a long time ago. It took me three successive Saturdays to steal the whole novel.

Francis Spufford, *The Child that Books Built* (2002).

Occasionally when we have opened some very attractive old book, we have stood reading for hours at the stall, lost in a brown study and worldly forgetfulness, and should probably have read on to the end of the last chapter, had not the vendor of published wisdom offered, in a satirically polite way, to bring us out a chair – 'Take a chair, sir; you must be tired.'

Leigh Hunt, *Retrospective Review* (*c*.1820).

*****

He set to work on a book, or a pyramid of books; his eyes glistening with an energy as fierce as that of the most sordid gold-digger who works at a rock of quartz, crushing his way through all impediments, no grain of the pure ore escaping his eager scrutiny. I called on him one morning at ten: he was in his study with a German folio open, resting on the broad marble mantelpiece, over an old-fashioned fire-place, and with a dictionary in his hand. He always read standing if possible. He had promised over night to go with me, but now begged me to let him off. I then rode to Leghorn, eleven or twelve miles distant, and passed the day there; on returning at six in the evening to dine with Mrs Shelley and the Williamses, as I had engaged to do, I went into the Poet's room and found him exactly in the position in which I had left him in the morning, but looking pale and exhausted.

'Well,' I said, 'have you found it?'

Shutting the book and going to the window, he replied, 'No, I have lost it': with a deep sigh: 'I have lost a day.'

'Cheer up, my lad, and come to dinner.'

Putting his long fingers through his masses of wild tangled hair, he answered faintly, 'You go, I have dined – late eating don't do for me.'

'What is this?' I asked, as I was going out of the room, pointing to one of his bookshelves with a plate containing bread and cold meat on it.

'That' – colouring – 'why, that must be my dinner. It's very foolish; I thought I had eaten it.'

Edward Trelawny, *Records of Shelley, Byron and the Author* (1878).

Before dinner Dr Johnson seized upon Mr Charles Sheridan's *Account of the late Revolution in Sweden*, and seemed to read it ravenously, as if he devoured it, which was to all appearance his method of studying. 'He knows how to read better than anyone (said Mrs Knowles;) he gets at the substance of a book directly; he tears the heart out of it.' He kept it wrapt up in the table-cloth in his lap during the time of dinner, from an avidity to have one entertainment in readiness when he should have finished another; resembling (if I may use so coarse a simile) a dog who holds a bone in his paws in reserve, while he eats something else which has been thrown to him.

James Boswell, *Life of Johnson* (1791).

COOKE

Why, hath he more bookes?

ANDREW

More than ten Marts send over.

BUTLER

And can he tell their names?

ANDREW

Their names? he has 'em
As perfect as his pater noster, but that's nothing,

> Has read them over leafe by leafe three thousand times;
> But here's the wonder, though their weight would sinke
> A Spanish Carracke, without other ballast,
> He carryeth them all in his head, and yet
> He walks upright.

BUTLER

> Surely he has a strong braine.

ANDREW

> If all thy pipes of wine were fill'd with bookes,
> Made of the barks of trees, or mysteries writ
> In old moth-eaten vellum, he would sip thy Cellar
> Dry, and still be thirsty; Then for's Diet,
> He eates and digests more Volumes at a meale,
> Than there would be Larks (though the sky should fall)
> Devowr'd in a moneth in *Paris*.

> John Fletcher, *The Elder Brother* (1624/5).

Dozens of my books were purchased with money which ought to have been spent upon what are called the necessaries of life. Many a time I have stood before a stall, or a bookseller's window, torn by conflict of intellectual desire and bodily need. At the very hour of dinner, when my stomach clamoured for food, I have been stopped by sight of a volume so long coveted, and marked at so advantageous a price, that I could not let it go; yet to buy it meant pangs of famine. My Heyne's *Tibullus* was grasped at such a moment. It lay on the stall of the old book-shop in Goodge Street – a stall where now and then one found an excellent thing among quantities of rubbish. Sixpence was the price – sixpence! At that time I used to eat my midday meal (of course my dinner) at a coffee-shop in Oxford Street, one of the real old coffee-shops, such as now, I suppose, can hardly be found. Sixpence was all I had – yes, all I had in the world; it would purchase a plate of meat and vegetables. But I did not dare to hope that the *Tibullus* would wait until the morrow, when a certain small sum fell due to me. I paced the pavement, fingering the coppers in my pocket, eyeing the stall, two appetites at combat within me. The book was bought and I went home with it, and as I made a dinner of bread and butter I gloated over the pages.

George Gissing, *The Private Papers of Henry Ryecroft* (1903).

He had given up reading. He had hardly opened a book since his misfortune. This may seem an odd thing to have to record about a gentleman, and to a certain extent a scholar; but so it was. He wanted to lower himself, and he was beginning to succeed. There was an essential honesty in him, which made him hate to appear what he was not; and this feeling, carried to an absurd extent, prevented his taking refuge in the most obvious remedy for all troubles except hunger – books. He did not know, as I do, that determined reading – reading of anything, even the advertisements in a newspaper – will stop all cravings except those of the stomach, and will even soften them; but he guessed it, nevertheless. 'Why should I read?' said he. 'I must learn to do as the rest of them.' And so he did as the rest of them, and 'rather loafed away his time than otherwise.'

Henry Kingsley, *Ravenshoe* (1862).

* * * * *

Unfortunately there was the problem that even if you read everything, you don't read it as the same person. When he first read *The Iliad*, the opening was just the opening: an explanation. The anger of Achilles: people always thought it referred to Achilles' rage at losing his favourite slave-girl or his sidekick Patroclus.

When he had read it first at eleven, he hadn't read it. At seventeen when he reapplied it was beginning to come into focus.

Yet only when he was thirty and he had been stuck in a lift, and had gone in for the third time had the meaning dripped through like portly raindrops infiltrating a roof.

Tibor Fischer, 'Bookcruncher' (2001).

Still, if the writing doesn't change, we do. We reread, sometimes, to test ourselves, to see who we've become. There are writers we tried too young. . . . Reading's so invisible an art, we forget that we've gotten better at it. Books still baffle us occasionally, but not nearly so often, and there are reasons for this bafflement – we're in a bum frame of mind, or the book's too technical for someone with our background, or maybe it's just written badly. In short, we've learned to know ourselves as readers. We've learned specific tricks, as well, how to adjust our reading style to the pages at hand. We slow-dance with some, others we ride like breaking waves. A few we don't go near without protective gear. It wasn't until I was loose in that no-man's-land after college that two of the more blindingly obvious illuminations struck me: That I couldn't read *every book* (and could leave off torturing myself). And that, life being short, I could just plain quit a book if I wanted. Blasphemy!

David Long, 'On rereading' (1987).

*****

Lavinia, go with me;
I'll to thy closet, and go read with thee
Sad stories chancèd in the times of old.
Come, boy, and go with me: thy sight is young,
And thou shalt read when mine begin to dazzle.

William Shakespeare, *Titus Andronicus* (1594).

Studio B was the snakebite studio at WLT, the tomb of the radio mummy, and bad things happened to people who went in there . . . On October 14th, 1937, Vince Upton did his *Story Hour with Grandpa Sam* in B, when C was closed for repairs after somebody punched out part of the wall. He plopped down in the 'old porch chair' and read off the names of the Happy Birthday club and picked the lucky winner of an all-day trip to Excelsior Amusement Park and said, 'Well, you young whippersnappers, how about you gather round for a good old-fashioned yarn?' and picked up his script and began to read. It didn't take him ten seconds to realize that he was in trouble. He had glanced at the script minutes before, and it looked okay, but now, instead of riding away to the Pecos to locate Sally and Skipper, Cowboy Chuck poured himself a stiff drink of – Vince made it root beer – and spat on the barroom floor and muttered, 'I come from St Paul, Minnesota, a city full of angry maudlin Irishmen and flabby chinless men with limp moustaches waving their shrivelled dicks at the cruel blue sky – and as soon as I was lucky enough to get in trouble there, I left town and started to see what life was all about,' though of course Vince left off the part about penises. 'Well, Cowboy Chuck is sure upset, isn't he,' Vince ad-libbed, waving to the empty control room. He pointed toward the turntable up beyond the big control room window, making circular motions, gave the *cut* sign, but nothing happened. Where was Gene?

He swallowed hard and ploughed forward. From St Paul, Cowboy Chuck had earned vast wealth in the whiskey trade in Chicago and moved in with a dark Paraguayan beauty named Pabletta, whose breasts were pale and small and shivered at the thrill of his touch. Slowly, his voice shaking with the effort, Vince picked his way through the story, glancing ahead as he read and skirting most of the worst parts, but some things he didn't catch until he already had said them – 'I slipped my pistol into her hot throbbing love nest' – and suddenly there were naked bodies slipping around in the sheets moaning and pounding the mattress and he had to edit on the run, condense, mumble, beat his way out of the underbrush, and toss in an occasional, 'Of course, I knew I should not have done this,' or 'Something told me that someday I would be punished for that.' Vince was a script man: the thought of speaking impromptu made him feel faint. Nonetheless, when Cowboy Chuck and Pabletta went swimming and Chuck stripped off the paper-thin white cotton shirt in which her taut nipples protruded like accusing fingers, Vince had to put down the script and improvise his way to shore. Cowboy Chuck ran out of the lake and put on his pants and rode to town and found a church. His mother was there, on her knees, scrubbing the floor. He knelt down and begged her forgiveness. He denounced the evil influence of modern novels. Word came, via a boy who rode up on his bicycle, that Pabletta had died beneath the wheels of a truck. Chuck called on all listeners, especially the kiddos, to obey their parents and attend church regularly, and then the big hand approached twelve, and the announcer said, 'That's all for today. Be sure to join Grandpa Sam tomorrow at the same time for another exciting story.' And it was all over.

Garrison Keillor, *Radio Romance* (1991).

In the winter of 1815–6, when the cold and the cost of candle-light would have detained me in bed, I was so fortunate as to discover an agreeable means of spending my mornings [Here he describes an acquaintance.] . . . If I pleased, he would introduce me to his occasional employer, the baker in Canal Street, who, he said, was passionately fond of reading, but without leisure for its gratification. If I would go early – very early – say five o'clock in the morning, and read aloud to him and his two sons, while they were preparing their batch, I should be regularly rewarded for my trouble with a penny roll newly drawn from the oven. . . . Behold me, then, quitting my lodgings in the West Port, before five o'clock in the winter mornings, and pursuing my way across the town to the cluster of sunk streets below the North Bridge, of which Canal Street was the principal. The scene of operations was a cellar of confined dimensions, reached by a flight of steps descending from the street, and possessing a small back window immediately beyond the baker's kneading-board. Seated on a folded-up sack in the sole of the window, with a book in one hand and a penny candle stuck in a bottle near the other, I went to work for the amusement of the company. The baker was not particular as to subject. All he stipulated was for something comic and laughable. Aware of his tastes, I tried him first with the jocularities of *Roderick Random*, which was a great success, and produced shouts of laughter. . . . My services as a reader for two and a half hours every morning were unfailingly recompensed by a donation of the anticipated roll, with which, after getting myself brushed of the flour, I went on my way to shop-opening, lamp-cleaning, and all the rest of it, at Calton Street.

William Chambers, *Memoir of Robert Chambers: with Autobiographic Reminiscences of William Chambers* (1872).

My mother had left some romances behind her, which my father and I began to read after supper. At first it was only a question of practicing me in reading by the aid of amusing books; but soon the interest became so lively, that we used to read in turns without stopping, and spent whole nights in this occupation. We were unable to leave off until the volume was finished. Sometimes, my father, hearing the swallows begin to twitter in the early morning, would say, quite ashamed, 'Let us go to bed; I am more of a child than yourself.'

Jean-Jacques Rousseau, *The Confessions* (1781).

My grandmother used to read aloud to me, chiefly the stories of Maria Edgeworth. There was one story in the book, called *The False Key*, which she said was not a very nice story, and she would therefore not read it to me. I read the whole story, a sentence at a time, in the course of bringing the book from the shelf to my grandmother.

Bertrand Russell, Autobiography (1967).

> One day,
> For our delight we read of Lancelot,
> How him love thrall'd. Alone we were, and no
> Suspicion near us. Oft-times by that reading
> Our eyes were drawn together, and the hue
> Fled from our alter'd cheek. But at one point
> Alone we fell. When of that smile we read,
> The wished smile, so rapturously kiss'd
> By one so deep in love, then he, who ne'er
> From me shall separate, at once my lips
> All trembling kiss'd. The book and writer both
> Were love's purveyors. In its leaves that day
> We read no more.

Dante Alighieri, Inferno, Canto V (begun 1307).

Grandpa and I must have pottered about in church almost every day, and the echoing spaces, the stained glass and the smell of Brasso, chrysanthemums, damp pew-oak and iron mould from the choir's surplices were heady compensations for isolation. He'd tell me stories and read me to sleep at night, when he'd often drop off first, stretched out on the couch, mouth open, snoring, his beaky profile lit up by the candle. In fact, he got so impatient with my favourite books (which both he and I knew by heart) that one momentous day, before I was four, he taught me to read in self-defence.

Lorna Sage, Bad Blood (2000).

Philip read in a high-pitched and unnatural tone of voice, which deprived the words of their reality; for even familiar expressions can become unfamiliar and convey no ideas, if the utterance is forced or affected. Philip was somewhat of a pedant; yet there was a simplicity in his pedantry not always to be met with in those who are self-taught, and which might have interested anyone who cared to know with what labour and difficulty he had acquired the knowledge which now he prized so highly; reading out Latin quotations as easily as if they were English, and taking a pleasure in rolling polysyllables, until all at once looking askance at Sylvia, he saw that her head had fallen back, her pretty rosy lips open, her eyes fast shut; in short, she was asleep.

Elizabeth Gaskell, *Sylvia's Lovers* (1863).

The Hilberys subscribed to a library, which delivered books on Tuesdays and Fridays, and Katharine did her best to interest her parents in the works of living and highly respectable authors; but Mrs Hilbery was perturbed by the very look of the light, gold-wreathed volumes, and would make little faces as if she tasted something bitter as the reading went on; while Mr Hilbery would treat the moderns with a curious elaborate banter such as one might apply to the antics of a promising child. So this evening, after five pages or so of one of these masters, Mrs Hilbery protested that it was all too clever and cheap and nasty for words.

'Please, Katharine, read us something *REAL*.'

Katharine had to go to the bookcase and choose a portly volume in sleek, yellow calf, which had directly a sedative effect upon both her parents. But the delivery of the evening post broke in upon the periods of Henry Fielding, and Katharine found that her letters needed all her attention.

Virginia Woolf, *Night and Day* (1919).

'Yes, she had her favourites, always one of the young ones who was weak and delicate, and she took them under her wing and made sure that they didn't have to work, got them better barracks space and took care of them and fed them better, and in the evenings she had them brought to her. And the girls were never allowed to say what she did with them in the evening, and we assumed she was . . . also because they all ended up on the transports, as if she had had her fun with them and then had got bored. But it wasn't like that at all, and one day one of them finally talked, and we learned that the girls read aloud to her, evening after evening after evening. That was better than if they . . . and better than working themselves to death on the building site. I must have thought it was better, or I couldn't have forgotten it. But was it better?'

Bernhard Schlink, *The Reader* (1997).

At last when Tony had passed six or seven consecutive nights without fever, Mr Todd said, 'Now I think you are well enough to see the books.'

At one end of the hut there was a kind of loft formed by a rough platform erected in the eaves of the roof. Mr Todd propped a ladder against it and mounted. Tony followed, still unsteady after his illness. Mr Todd sat on the platform and Tony stood at the top of the ladder looking over. There was a heap of bundles there, tied up with rag, palm leaf and raw hide.

'It has been hard to keep out the worms and ants. Two are practically destroyed. But there is an oil the Indians make that is useful.'

He unwrapped the nearest parcel and handed down a calf-bound book. It was an early American edition of *Bleak House*.

'It does not matter which we take first.'

'You are fond of Dickens?'

'Why, yes, of course. More than fond, far more. You see, they are the only books I have ever heard. My father used to read them and then later the black man . . . and now you. I had heard them all several times by now but I never get tired; there is always more to be learned and notice, so many characters, so many changes of scene, so many words . . . I have all Dickens's books here except those that the ants devoured. It takes a long time to read them all – more than two years.'

'Well,' said Tony lightly, 'they will well last out my visit.'

'Oh, I hope not. It is delightful to start again. Each time I think I find more to enjoy and admire.'

They took down the first volume of *Bleak House* and that afternoon Tony had his first reading.

He had always rather enjoyed reading aloud and in the first year of marriage had shared several books in this way with Brenda, until one day, in a moment of frankness, she remarked that it was torture to her. He had read to John Andrew, late in the afternoon, in winter, while the child was before the nursery fender eating his supper. But Mr Todd was a unique audience.

The old man sat astride his hammock opposite Tony, fixing him throughout with his eyes, and following the words, soundlessly, with his lips. Often when a new character was introduced he would say, 'Repeat the name, I have forgotten him,' or 'Yes, yes, I remember her well. She dies, poor woman.' He would frequently interrupt with questions; not as Tony would have imagined about the circumstances of the story – such things as the procedure of the Lord Chancellor's Court or the social conventions of the time, though they must have been unintelligible, did not concern him – but always about the characters. 'Now, why does she say that? Does she really mean it? Did she feel faint because of the heat of the fire or of something in that paper?' He laughed loudly at all the jokes and at some passages which did not seem humorous to

Tony, asking him to repeat them two or three times, and later at the description of the sufferings of the outcasts in 'Tom-all-alone's' tears ran down his cheeks into his beard. His comments on the story were usually simple. 'I think that Dedlock is a very proud man,' or 'Mrs Jellyby does not take enough care of her children.'

Tony enjoyed the readings almost as much as he did.

At the end of the first day the old man said, 'You read beautifully, with a far better accent than the black man. And you explain better. It is almost as though my father were here again.' And always at the end of a session he thanked his guest courteously. 'I enjoyed that *very* much. It was an extremely distressing chapter. But, if I remember it rightly, it will all turn out well.'

By the time they were in the second volume, however, the novelty of the old man's delight had begun to wane, and Tony was feeling strong enough to be restless. He touched more than once on the subject of his departure, asking about canoes and rains and the possibility of finding guides. But Mr Todd seemed obtuse and paid no attention to these hints.

One day, running his thumb through the pages of *Bleak House* that remained to be read, Tony said, 'We still have a lot to get through. I hope I shall be able to finish it before I go.'

'Oh yes,' said Mr Todd. 'Do not disturb yourself about that. You will have time to finish it, my friend.'

For the first time Tony noticed something slightly menacing in his host's manner. That evening at supper, a brief meal of farine and dried beef, eaten just before sundown, Tony renewed the subject.

'You know, Mr Todd, the time has come when I must be thinking about getting back to civilization. I have already imposed myself on your hospitality far too long.'

Mr Todd bent over the plate, crunching mouthfuls of farine, but made no reply.

'How soon do you think I shall be able to get a boat? . . . I said how soon do you think I shall be able to get a boat? I appreciate all your kindness to me more than I can say, but . . .'

'My friend, any kindness I may have shown is amply repaid by your reading of Dickens. Do not let us mention the subject again.'

'Well, I'm very glad you have enjoyed it. I have, too. But I really must be thinking of getting back . . .'

'Yes,' said Mr Todd. 'The black man was like that. He thought of it all the time. But he died here . . .'

Twice during the next day Tony opened the subject but his host was evasive. Finally he said, 'Forgive me, Mr Todd, but I really must press the point. When can I get a boat?'

'There is no boat.'

'Well, the Indians can build one.'

'You must wait for the rains. There is not enough water in the river now.'

'How long will that be?'

'A month . . . two months . . .'

They had finished *Bleak House* and were nearing the end of *Dombey and Son,* when the rain came.

'Now it is time to make preparations to go.'

'Oh, that is impossible. The Indians will not make a boat during the rainy season – it is one of their superstitions.'

'You might have told me.'

'Did I not mention it? I forgot.'

. . .

They finished *Dombey and Son*; nearly a year had passed since Tony had left England, and his gloomy foreboding of permanent exile became suddenly acute when, between the pages of *Martin Chuzzlewit*, he found a document written in pencil in irregular characters.

Year 1919
I James Todd of Brazil do swear to Barnabas Washington
of Georgetown that if he finish this book in fact *Martin
Chuzzlewit* I will let him go away back as soon as finished.

There followed a heavy pencil X and after it: Mr Todd
made this mark signed Barnabas Washington.

'Mr Todd,' said Tony, 'I must speak frankly. You saved my
life, and when I get back to civilization I will reward you to
the best of my ability. I will give you anything within reason.
But at present you are keeping me here against my will. I
demand to be released.'

'But, my friend, what is keeping you? You are under no
restraint. Go when you like.'

'You know very well that I can't get away without your
help.'

'In that case you must humour an old man. Read me
another chapter.'

'Mr Todd, I swear by anything you like that when I get to
Manáos I will find someone to take my place. I will pay a man
to read to you all day.'

'But I have no need of another man. You read so well.'

'I have read for the last time.'

'I hope not,' said Mr Todd politely.

That evening at supper only one plate of dried meat and
farine was brought in and Mr Todd ate alone. Tony lay
without speaking, staring at the thatch.

Next day at noon a single plate was put before Mr Todd
but with it lay his gun, cocked, on his knee, as he ate. Tony
resumed the reading of *Martin Chuzzlewit* where it had been
interrupted.

Weeks passed hopelessly. They read *Nicholas Nickleby* and
Little Dorrit and *Oliver Twist*. Then a stranger arrived in the
savannah, a half-caste prospector . . . Mr Todd was vexed at

his arrival, gave him farine and *tasso* and sent him on his journey within an hour of his arrival, but in that hour Tony had time to scribble his name on a slip of paper and put it into the man's hand. . . .

The weeks passed; there was no sign of rescue but Tony endured the day for hope of what might happen the morrow; he even felt a slight stirring of cordiality towards his jailer and was therefore quite willing to join him when, one evening after a long conference with an Indian neighbour, he proposed a celebration.

'It is one of the local feast days,' he explained, 'and they have been making *piwari*. You may not like it but you should try some.' . . .

Tony gulped the dark liquid, trying not to taste it . . . He leant back in the hammock feeling unusually contented . . . Then he shut his eyes and thought of England and Hetton and fell asleep.

He woke, still in the Indian hut, with the impression that he had outslept his usual hour. . . . He looked for his watch and found to his surprise that it was not on his wrist. . . . When he reached the house he found Mr Todd sitting there.

'Ah, my friend, you are late for the reading this afternoon. There is scarcely another half hour of light. How do you feel?'

'Rotten. That drink doesn't seem to agree with me.'

'I will give you something to make you feel better. The forest has remedies for everything; to make you awake and to make you sleep.'

'You haven't seen my watch anywhere?'

'You have missed it?'

'Yes. I thought I was wearing it. I say, I've never slept so long.'

'Not since you were a baby. Do you know how long? Two days.'

'Nonsense, I can't have.'

'Yes, indeed. It is a long time. It is a pity because you missed our guests.'

'Guests?'

'Why yes. I have been quite gay while you were asleep. Three men from outside. Englishmen. It is a pity you missed them. A pity for them, too, as they particularly wished to see you. But what could I do? You were so sound asleep. They had come all the way to find you, so – I thought you would not mind – as you could not greet them yourself, I gave them a little souvenir, your watch. . . . They were very pleased with it. And they took some photographs of the little cross I put up to commemorate your coming. They were pleased with that too. They were very easily pleased. But I do not suppose they will visit us again, our life here is so retired . . . no pleasures except reading . . . I do not suppose we shall ever have visitors again . . . We will not have any Dickens today . . . but tomorrow, and the day after that, and the day after that. Let us read *Little Dorrit* again. There are passages in that book I can never hear without the temptation to weep.'

Evelyn Waugh, *A Handful of Dust* (1934).

2. 'TRUST THEIR TRUTH':
THE QUALITIES OF BOOKS

No lover of good books – in other words no cultured person – can feel continuous hostility to another reader of the same sort. The mere sight of that engrossed look, that absorbed and rapt delight, would, one may well suppose, disarm the most vindictive hate.

John Cowper Powys, *The Meaning of Culture* (1929).

And as for me, although my wit is small,
I find that books most happily enthral;
That I so reverence them in my heart,
So trust their truth, so pleasure in their art,
That there is scarce a single joy I know
That can persuade me from my books to go.

Geoffrey Chaucer, *The Legend of Good Women* (c.1385–6).

To divert myself from a troublesome fancy 'tis but to run to my books; they presently fix me to them, and drive the other out of my thoughts; and do not mutiny to see that I have only recourse to them for want of other, more real, natural and lively conveniences; they always receive me with the same kindness.

Michel de Montaigne, 'The Commerce of Reading' (1580).

Books admitted me to their world open-handedly, as people, for the most part, did not. The life I lived in books was one of ease and freedom, worldly wisdom, glitter, dash and style. I loved its intimacy, too – the way in which I could expose to books all the private feelings that I had to shield from the frosty and contemptuous outside world. In books you could hope beyond hope, be heartbroken, love, pity, admire, even cry, all without shame.

No author ever despised me. They made me welcome in their books, never joked about my asthma and generally behaved as if I was the best company in the world. For this I worshipped them. I read and read and read – under the bed-clothes with an illegal torch, surreptitiously in lessons with an open book on my knees, through long cathedral sermons, prep, and on the muddy touchlines ('*Kill* him, Owen') of rugby pitches, to which I was drafted as a supporter.

Jonathan Raban, *For Love and Money* (1987).

'There is nothing like books'; – of all things sold incomparably the cheapest, of all pleasures the least palling, they take up little room, keep quiet when they are not wanted, and, when taken up, bring us face to face with the choicest men who have ever lived, at their choicest moments.

As my walking companion in the country, I was so UnEnglish (excuse the two capitals) as on the whole, to prefer my pocket Milton which I carried for twenty years, to the not unbeloved bull terrier Trimmer, who accompanied me for five – for Milton never fidgeted, frightened horses, ran after sheep or got run over by a goods-van.

Samuel Palmer, letter to Charles West Cape, 31 January, 1880.

For him, books were like friends, and reading an extension of companionship – a way of expanding beyond the circumference of time and place the circle of one's kindred acquaintances.

Michael Holroyd, *Lytton Strachey: A Biography* (1971).

Outside a dog, a book is a man's best friend. Inside a dog, it's too dark to read.

Groucho Marx, apocryphal.

There is no mistaking a real book when one meets it. It is like falling in love, and like that colossal adventure it is an experience of great social import. Even as the tranced swain, the booklover yearns to tell others of his bliss. He writes letters about it, adds it to the postscript of all manner of communications, intrudes it into telephone messages, and insists on his friends writing down the title of his find. Like the simple-hearted betrothed, once certain of his conquest, 'I want you to love her, too!' It is a jealous passion also. He feels a little indignant if he finds that anyone else has discovered the book also. He sees an enthusiastic review – very likely in *The New Republic* – and says, with great scorn, 'I read the book three months ago.' There are even some perversions of passion by which a booklover loses much of his affection for his pet if he sees it too highly commended by some rival critic.

Christopher Morley, 'On visiting bookshops' (1925).

Occasionally I come across a book which I feel has been written especially for me and for me only. Like a jealous lover, I don't want anybody else to hear of it. To have a million such readers, unaware of each other's existence, to be read with passion and never talked about, is the daydream, surely, of every author.

W. H. Auden, 'Reading' (1963).

Never think of marriage and if the thought should occur, take down a book and begin to read until it vanishes.

Isaac Gossett, quoted by A. N. L. Munby, in 'Some caricatures of book-collectors: an essay' (1948).

* * * * *

To read good books is like holding a conversation with the most eminent minds of past centuries and, moreover, a studied conversation in which these authors reveal to us only the best of their thoughts.

René Descartes, *Discourse on Method* (1637).

The importance of reading, not slight stuff to get through the time, but the best that has been written, forces itself upon me more and more every year I live; it is living in good company, the best company, and people are generally keen enough, or too keen, about doing that, yet they will not do it in the simplest and most innocent manner, by reading.

Matthew Arnold, letter to Frances Arnold, 1 January, 1882.

* * * * *

. . . you may be strenuously advised to *keep* reading. Any good book, any book that is wiser than yourself, will teach you something – a great many things, indirectly and directly, if your mind be open to learn.

Thomas Carlyle, 'On a proper choice of reading' (1843).

Of all the inanimate objects, of all men's creation, books are the nearest to us, for they contain our very thoughts, our ambitions, our indignations, our illusions, our fidelity to truth, and our persistent leaning towards error. But most of all they resemble us in their precarious hold on life.

Joseph Conrad, 'Books' (1905).

The knowledge of the world is only to be acquired in the world, and not in a closet. Books alone will never teach it you; but they will suggest many things to your observation, which might otherwise escape you; and your own observations upon mankind, when compared with those which you will find in books, will help you to fix the true point.

Lord Chesterfield, letter to his son, 4 October, 1746.

Books say: she did this because. Life says: she did this. Books are where things are explained to you; life is where things aren't. I'm not surprised some people prefer books. Books make sense of life. The only problem is that the lives they make sense of are other people's lives, never your own.

Julian Barnes, *Flaubert's Parrot* (1984).

*****

For some reason or other the effect of long absorption in reading . . . is to purge the mind of annoying and teasing thoughts and leave us amiable, genial, benevolent.

John Cowper Powys, *The Meaning of Culture* (1929).

'Don't you think you might tell me what you've been up to all the time you've been in Paris?'

'I've been reading a good deal. Eight or ten hours a day. I've attended lectures at the Sorbonne. I think I've read everything that's important in French literature and I can read Latin, at least Latin prose, almost as easily as I can read French. Of course Greek's more difficult. But I have a very good teacher. Until you came here I used to go to him three evenings a week.'

'And what is that going to lead to?'

'The acquisition of knowledge,' he smiled.

'It doesn't sound very practical.'

'Perhaps it isn't and on the other hand perhaps it is. But it's enormous fun. You can't imagine what a thrill it is to read the *Odyssey* in the original. It makes you feel as if you had only to get on tiptoe and stretch out your hands to touch the stars.'

He got up from his chair, as though impelled by an excitement that seized him, and walked up and down the small room.

'I've been reading Spinoza the last month or two. I don't suppose I understand very much of it yet, but it fills me with exultation. It's like landing from your plane on a great plateau in the mountains. Solitude, and an air so pure that it goes to your head like wine and you feel like a million dollars.'

W. Somerset Maugham, *The Razor's Edge* (1944).

Taking up a book like Arnauld, and reading a chapter of his lively, manly sense, is like throwing your manuals, and scalpels, and microscopes, and natural (most unnatural) orders out of your hand and head, and taking a game with the Grange Club, or a run to the top of Arthur Seat. Exertion quickens your pulse, expands your lungs, makes your blood warmer and redder, fills your mouth with the pure waters of relish, strengthens and supples your legs; and though on your way to the top you may encounter rocks, and baffling *débris*, and gusts of fierce winds rushing out upon you from behind corners, just as you will find in Arnauld, and all truly serious and honest books of the kind, difficulties and puzzles, winds of doctrines, and deceitful mists; still you are rewarded at the top by the wide view. You see, as from a tower, the end of all. You look into the perfections and relations of things. You see the clouds, the bright lights, and the everlasting hills on the far horizon. You come down the hill a happier, a better, and a hungrier man, and of a better mind. But, as we said, you must eat the book, you must crush it, and cut it with your teeth and swallow it; just as you must walk up, and not be carried up the hill, much less imagine you are there, or look upon a picture of what you would see were you up, however accurately or artistically done; no – you yourself must *do* both.

John Brown, 'With brains, Sir!' (1861).

* * * * *

In a very real sense, then, people who have read good literature have lived more than people who cannot or will not read. To have read *Gulliver's Travels* is to have had the experience, with Jonathan Swift, of turning sick at one's stomach at the conduct of the human race; to read *Huckleberry Finn* is to feel what it is like to drift down the Mississippi River on a raft; to have read Byron is to have suffered with him his rebellions and neuroses and to have enjoyed with him his nose-thumbing at society; to have read *Native Son* is to know how it feels to be frustrated in the particular way in which many Negroes in Chicago are frustrated. This is the great task that affective communication performs: it enables us to feel how others felt about life, even if they lived thousands of miles away and centuries ago. It is not true that we have only one life to live; if we can read, we can live as many more lives and as many kinds of lives as we wish.

S. I. Hayakawa, *Language in Thought and Action* (1952).

* * * * *

The love of books cannot be acquired. It must be born in one, like the love of music, the love of horses, or the love of the sea (or, to take a humbler instance, a taste for olives).

George W. E. Russell, 'Books' (1914).

3. 'HAVING SO PREPARED HIMSELF': SETTLING DOWN TO READ

... there is nothing more fit to be looked at than the outside of a book. It is, as I may say, from repeated experience, a pure and unmixed pleasure to have a goodly volume lying before you, and to know that you may open it if you please, and need not open it unless you please.

Thomas Love Peacock, *Crotchet Castle* (1831).

You turn the book over in your hands, you scan the sentences on the back of the jacket, generic phrases that don't say a great deal. So much the better, there is no message that indiscreetly outshouts the message that the book itself must communicate directly, that you must extract from the book, however much or little it may be. Of course, this circling of the book, too, this reading around it before reading inside it, is a part of the pleasure in a new book, but like all preliminary pleasures, it has its optimal duration if you want it to serve as a thrust toward the more substantial pleasure of the consummation of the act, namely the reading of the book.

Italo Calvino, *If on a Winter's Night a Traveller* (1979).

Oh, delightful! To cut open the leaves, to inhale the fragrancy of the scarcely dry paper, to examine the type to see who is the printer (which is some clue to the value that is set upon the work), to launch out into regions of thought and invention never trod until now, and to explore characters that never met a human eye before – this is a luxury worth sacrificing a dinner-party, or a few hours of a spare morning to.

William Hazlitt, 'On reading new books' (1839).

That evening he unpacked his books from London. The box was full of things he had been waiting for impatiently; a new volume of Herbert Spencer, another collection of the prolific Alphonse Daudet's brilliant tales, and a novel called *Middlemarch*, as to which there had lately been interesting things said in the reviews. He had declined three dinner invitations in favour of this feast.

Edith Wharton, *The Age of Innocence* (1920).

In my grandmother's room, the books were lying down; she used to borrow them from the lending-library and I never saw more than two at a time. These trashy works reminded me of New Year sweetmeats because their shiny flexible covers seemed to be cut out of glazed paper. Bright, white, almost new, they served as an excuse for petty mysteries. Each Friday, my grandmother would get dressed to go out and say: 'I'm going to take *them* back'; when she returned, and had taken off her black hat and veil, she would take *them* out of her muff and I would wonder, mystified: 'Are they the same ones?' She used to 'cover' them carefully and then, having chosen one, she would settle herself by the window, in her winged armchair, put on her spectacles, sigh with pleasure and weariness, and lower her eyelids with a delicately voluptuous smile which I have since discovered on the lips of the Mona Lisa.

Jean-Paul Sartre, *Words* (1964).

* * * * *

The bells out in the city rang a quarter to five, and I sat with the cocoa and bread and cheese hot inside me till five o'clock, when I started my cell task.

I had to side three mailbags, and it was easy enough to do, now that I had done a few days at it (not that I was a natural sewer), and I was looking forward to *Under the Greenwood Tree*, when I would be done; so I was fairly quick and when the bags were finished I shoved my chair back from the door a bit and turned into the table, stuck my legs in the mailbag, pulled it tight about me, and when I opened the book on the table I put my hands down under the bag and was warm all over, though the air of the winter night was black cold and blunt as metal.

Brendan Behan, Borstal Boy (1958).

The book was delivered to me in loose-leaf sections in the exercise yard. Karl-Heinz would tear some pages out – twenty or thirty – fold them up and stuff them in a crack in the palisade well. It was easy for me to retrieve them, hide them on my person and take them back to my cell undiscovered. I will never forget my excitement that first day as I prised the folded wad of pages from between the planks. Later, locked back in my cell I stuffed all but the first page into my mattress. If anyone came in I would have time to crumple up the page I was reading and pocket it.

I was ready to start. I sat down on my chair and spread the page flat before me on the table. The page was small, so was the type, as if it came from an octavo pocket edition. The paper was thin, like bible-paper. My hands were visibly trembling as I smoothed out the folds. I shut my eyes and paused before reading the first sentence. I felt humbled with gratitude. Karl-Heinz had given me only the text – I did not know the title, I did not know the author. I was ignorant of the book's subject or genre. Yet to me sitting there in that cell it felt as though I was on the brink of a fabulous adventure and that I held something immensely precious in my shaking hands. It was a divine moment. It was going to change my life.

'Chapter One'.

My heart beat vigorously with anticipation. The first sentences, the first paragraph . . . what would they be like? I read

I am now entering on a task which is without precedent and which when achieved will have no imitator. I am going to show my fellow creatures a man in all the integrity of nature; and that man shall be myself.

Yes. Myself! I know my own heart and have studied mankind. I am not made like anyone I have seen. I do not believe there is another man like me in existence.

I had to set the page down, such was my emotion. My heart clubbed, struggled violently in my chest. My God . . . I felt drugged, intoxicated, almost swooning.

I know I was in every possible way in reduced circumstances. Like a parched man in the desert coming across a spring of fresh water. But I have never read such an opening to a book, have never been so powerfully and immediately engaged. Who was this man? Whose was this voice that spoke to me so directly, whose brazen immodesty rang with such candid integrity? I read on, mesmerized. Ten pages were all Karl-Heinz had supplied this time. I read and re-read them. But the suspense was insufferable, agonizing. I had to wait two restless days for the next instalment.

Karl-Heinz 'fed' me the entire book over the next seven weeks. The metaphor is exact. The thin wads of pages were like crucial scraps of nutrition. I devoured them. I masticated, swallowed and digested that book. I cracked its bones and sipped its marrow; every fibre of meat, every cartilaginous nodule of gristle was dined on with gourmandizing fervour. I have never read before or since with such miserly love and profound concentration. I paid for half that book with lingering chaste kisses but the remaining portion was purchased more orthodoxly. I received my first Red Cross parcel. There had been some pilfering but I was left with a scarf, a pair of socks, a one-pound plum pudding and a bag of peppermints. Parcels began to arrive once a fortnight. I gave away my food for a book.

William Boyd, *The New Confessions* (1987).

They did not give me any light and took the candles away with them – and I had no money to buy any. So I began to scrape wax from the candlesticks, collecting it in a sardine tin, into which I poured some of the lamp oil. I made a wick by twisting some threads together and lit it from the stove; it burned with a smoky flame. When I turned one of the pages over in a very large book the red tongue of the wick flickered and threatened to go out and every minute it sank deeper into the evil-smelling pool of molten wax. The acrid smoke stung my eyes but the pleasure I derived from looking at the illustrations and reading the captions more than compensated for all these discomforts. Those illustrations made the world a larger place, beautifying it with fabulous towns, showing me high mountains and wonderful sea shores. Life blossomed miraculously, the earth became more attractive, richer in people and towns and many different things.

Maxim Gorky, *My Apprenticeship* (1915).

* * * * *

I remember a Saturday when I was the only person in the library. I took out Faulkner's *Absalom, Absalom!* (buff paper, good typography) and went back to my room. I felt, somehow, with everybody else out partying, Faulkner deserved my best. I showered, washed my hair, put on fresh clothes, and with one of Bob Loomis's wooden-tipped cigars, for the wickedness of it, made myself comfortable and opened the Faulkner to hear Miss Rosa Coldfield telling Quentin Compson about Thomas Sutpen.

Guy Davenport, 'On reading' (1987).

After breakfast, on the morning of which we are writing, the archdeacon, as usual, retired to his study, intimating that he was going to be very busy . . . On entering this sacred room he carefully opened the paper case on which he was wont to compose his favourite sermons, and spread on it a fair sheet of paper, and one partly written on; then he placed his ink-stand, looked at his pen, and folded his blotting-paper; having done so, he got up again from his seat, stood with his back to the fireplace, and yawned comfortably, stretching out vastly his huge arms, and opening his burly chest. He then walked across the room and locked the door; and having so prepared himself, he threw himself into his easy chair, took from a secret drawer beneath his table a volume of *Rabelais*, and began to amuse himself with the witty mischief of Panurge; and so passed the archdeacon's morning on that day.

Anthony Trollope, *The Warden* (1855).

The foundation of her knowledge was really laid in the idleness of her grandmother's house, where, as most of the other inmates were not reading people, she had uncontrolled use of a library full of books with frontispieces, which she used to climb upon a chair to take down. When she had found one to her taste – she was guided in the selection chiefly by the frontispiece – she carried it into a mysterious apartment which lay beyond the library and which was called, traditionally, no one knew why, the office. Whose office it had been and at what period it had flourished, she never learned; it was enough for her that it contained an echo and a pleasant musty smell and that it was a chamber of disgrace for old pieces of furniture whose infirmities were not always apparent (so that the disgrace seemed unmerited and rendered them victims of injustice) and with which, in the manner of children, she had established relations almost human, certainly dramatic.

Henry James, *The Portrait of a Lady* (1881).

On every landing there were long benches, covered with green velvet, where it was delightful to lie on one's stomach and read. But one was still more comfortable between the second and last floors, sitting on the steps themselves, which were laid with a black and white speckled carpet, bordered with wide strips of red. The light that fell from the glass roof was soft and peaceful. I sat on one step and leant my elbow on the one above, which also served as a reading desk, as it slowly dug into my ribs.

André Gide, *If it Die* (1920).

My favourite place for reading was the loft behind the yard. Except when Father was getting out fresh sacks of grain it was the quietest place in the house. There were huge piles of sacks to lie on, and a sort of plastery smell mixed up with the smell of sainfoin, and bunches of cobwebs in all the corners, and just over the place where I used to lie there was a hole in the ceiling and a lath sticking out of the plaster. I can feel the feeling of it now. A winter day, just warm enough to lie still. I'm lying on my belly with *Chums* open in front of me. A mouse runs up the side of a sack like a clock-work toy, then suddenly stops dead and watches me with his little eyes like tiny jet beads. I'm twelve years old, but I'm Donovan the Dauntless. Two thousand miles up the Amazon I've just pitched my tent, and the roots of the mysterious orchid that blooms once in a hundred years are safe in the tin box under my camp bed. In the forests all round the Hopi-Hopi Indians, who paint their teeth scarlet and skin white men alive, are beating their war-drums. I'm watching the mouse and the mouse is watching me, and I can smell the dust and the sainfoin and the cool plastery smell, and I'm up the Amazon, and it's bliss, pure bliss.

George Orwell, *Coming up for Air* (1939).

A small breakfast-room adjoined the drawing-room: I slipped in there. It contained a bookcase: I soon possessed myself of a volume, taking care that it should be one stored with pictures. I mounted into the window-seat: gathering up my feet, I sat cross-legged, like a Turk; and, having drawn the red moreen curtain nearly close, I was shrined in double retirement.

Folds of scarlet drapery shut in my view to the right hand; to the left were the clear panes of glass, protecting, but not separating me from the drear November day. At intervals, while turning over the leaves of my book, I studied the aspect of that winter afternoon. Afar, it offered a pale blank of mist and cloud; near, a scene of wet lawn and storm-beat shrub, with ceaseless rain sweeping away wildly before a long and lamentable blast.

Charlotte Brontë, *Jane Eyre* (1847).

When I was a boy, and was known to be fond of reading, many patronizing adults assured me that there was nothing I liked better than to 'curl up with a book'. I despised them. I have never curled. My physique is not formed for it. It is a matter of legend that Abraham Lincoln read lying on his stomach in front of the fire; you should try that in order to understand the extraordinary indifference to physical comfort that Lincoln possessed. I have read about children who 'creep away into the attic' to read, and Victorian children's stories are full of children who cannot read anywhere except in a deeply embrasured window seat. You have to find your own best place for reading, and for most of us in the Western world it is sitting on a chair with a decent light – though for Lincolnians, of course, firelight is the thing. I have forgotten those people of whom it is said that they 'always have their noses in a book'. This makes reading difficult, but as I have said, you must suit yourself.

Robertson Davies, 'Reading' (1990).

Ada took a book from her bedside table and went into the upper hall and sat in the stuffed chair she had pulled from Monroe's bedroom and situated to catch the good light from the hall window. She had spent much of the past three damp months sitting in the chair reading, a quilt wrapped around her to hold back the chill of the house even in July. The books she had drawn from the shelves that summer had been varied and haphazard, little but recent novels, whatever she happened to pick up from Monroe's study. Trifles like *Sword and Gown* by Lawrence and many others of its type. She could read such books and a day later not know what they had been about. When she had read more notable books, the harsh fates of their doomed heroines served only to deepen her gloom. For a time, every book she plucked from the shelves frightened her, their contents all concerning mistakes made by wretched dark-haired women so that they ended their days punished, exiled, and alien. She had gone straight from *The Mill on the Floss* to a slim and troubling tale by Hawthorne on somewhat the same theme. Monroe had apparently not finished it, for the pages were uncut beyond the third chapter. She guessed Monroe would have thought the book unnecessarily grim, but to Ada it seemed good practice for her coming world. No matter what the book, though, the characters all seemed to lead fuller lives than she did.

At first, all she liked about the reading spot was the comfortable chair and the good light, but over the months she came to appreciate that the window's view offered some relief against the strain of such bleak stories, for when she looked up from the page, her eye swept across the fields and rose on waves of foggy ridges to the blue bulk of Cold Mountain.

Charles Frazier, *Cold Mountain* (1997).

But the grand device of a lover of books, whatever his creed, is to mingle his pleasure in reading with the other pleasures of his life. Deep and subtle are the various sensations that come to us in this way. Perhaps the most wonderful of all thoughts . . . are the thoughts that come to us when we have been reading some particularly thrilling book and then stop for a second to observe the shadows on the hills, or to look out upon the lights of the streets, or to gaze down at the sea.

John Cowper Powys, *The Meaning of Culture* (1929).

There are no days of my childhood which I lived so fully perhaps as those I thought I had left behind without living them, those I spent with a favourite book. Everything which, it seemed, filled them for others, but which I pushed aside as a vulgar impediment to a heavenly pleasure: the game for which a friend came to fetch me at the most interesting passage, the troublesome bee or shaft of sunlight which forced me to look up from the page or to change my position, the provisions for tea which I had been made to bring and which I had left beside me on the seat, untouched, while, above my head, the sun was declining in strength in the blue sky, the dinner for which I had had to return home and during which my one thought was to go upstairs straight away afterwards, and finish the rest of the chapter: reading should have prevented me from seeing all this as anything except importunity, but, on the contrary, so sweet is the memory it engraved in me (and so much more precious in my present estimation than what I then read so lovingly) that if still, today, I chance to leaf through these books from the past, it is simply as the only calendars I have preserved of those bygone days, and in the hope of finding reflected in their pages the houses and the ponds which no longer exist.

Marcel Proust, 'Days of Reading I' (1905).

* * * * *

A little before you go to sleep read something that is exquisite.
Desiderius Erasmus, *Colloquies: Of the Method of Study*,
(*c.*1500–8).

Only one hour in the normal day is more pleasurable than
the hour spent in bed with a book before going to sleep, and
that is the hour spent in bed with a book after being called in
the morning.
Rose Macaulay, *A Casual Commentary* (1925).

I . . . kiss my small son good night, and climb into my bed,
free to read anything I want, for hours. It is an ornate affair,
my bed, picked up for ten dollars from some *junque* shop
beside an Arkansas highway fifteen years ago, and it requires
four fat pillows to keep its medallions from printing their
whorls on my spine. But imagine – four fat pillows, a quilt
worn soft drawn up under my arms, the hood of yellow light,
the rose-coloured walls, Stieglitz' *Flatiron* in its dusky mist of
gum bichromate evoking the comforting sound of wheels on
wet pavement, my husband's closet open and spilling ties.
And on my bedside table whatever book I choose. I am a child
again, propped up on the sofa, sick and home from school.
My husband is kind – he brings me coffee soothed with milk;
he is a reader too, and he understands that reading is, in the
act itself, a sensory delight.
Lee Zacharias, 'In the Garden of the Word' (1990).

'LIGHTS OUT!' my father would scream.
I was reading the Russians now, reading Turgenev and
Gorky. My father's rule was that all lights were to be out by
8 p.m. . . .

*'All right, that's enough of those god-damned books!
Lights out!'*

To me, these men who had come into my life from nowhere
were my only chance. They were the only voices that spoke to
me.

'All right,' I would say.

Then I took the reading lamp, crawled under the blanket,
pulled the pillow under there, and read each new book, prop-
ping it against the pillow, under the quilt. It got very hot, the
lamp got hot, and I had trouble breathing. I would lift the
quilt for air.

'What's that? Do I see a light? Henry, are your lights out?'

I would quickly lower the quilt again and wait until I heard
my father snoring.

Turgenev was a very serious fellow but he could make me
laugh because a truth first encountered can be very funny.
When someone else's truth is the same as your truth, and he
seems to be saying it just for you, that's great.

I read my books at night, like that, under the quilt with the
overheated reading lamp. Reading all those good lines while
suffocating. It was magic.

Charles Bukowski, *Ham on Rye* (1982).

Hundreds and thousands, possibly millions, of people
every night in England read something in bed. They say
nothing about it except, 'I read for a little last night and then
slept like a top,' or 'I didn't feel like going to sleep last night,
so I read for a bit,' or 'I began reading so-and-so in bed last
night, and damn the book, I couldn't get to sleep until I finished it.' Usually nothing at all is said; if anything is said it is
very little. Yet what a large slice of each of our lives has gone
in this harmless occupation. We get our clothes off. We get
our pyjamas on. We wind our watches. We arrange the table
and the light and get into bed. We pile up, or double up, the

pillows. Then we settle down to it. Sometimes the book is so exciting that all thought of sleep fades away, and we read on oblivious of everything except the unseen menace in that dark house, the boat gliding stealthily along that misty river, the Chinaman's eyes peering through that greenish-yellow fog, or the sudden crack of the revolver in that den of infamy. Sometimes we read for a while and then feel as though we could go peacefully to sleep. Sometimes we struggle desperately to gum our failing attention to the acute analysis and safe deductions of our author. Our eyes squint and swim. Our head dizzies. We feel drunk, and, dropping the book aside from lax hands, just manage to get the light out before falling back into a dense and miry slumber. We all know these fights against inevitable sleep, those resolves to reach the inaccessible end of the chapter, those swimmings in the head, those relapses into the gulf of oblivion. And we all know those long readings when the mystery and suspense of the text so excite us that every creak of the stair and every fluttering of the pertinacious moths makes the heart stand still, and then keeps it beating hard for minutes. We have all turned the light out just in time; and we have all turned it out from boredom, or in an access of determined common-sense, and then turned it on again to resume the dreary reading where we left the piece of paper or the pencil in the page. But we seldom talk about it. It is part of our really private lives.

J. C. Squire, 'Reading in bed' (1927).

If that isn't insulting a wife to bring a book to bed, I don't know what wedlock is.

Douglas Jerrold, *Mrs Caudle's Curtain Lectures* (1894).

* * * * *

... all fellow readers who have ever taken a book along to a humble restaurant will understand my saying that life has few enjoyments as stoical and pure as reading Spinoza's *Ethics*, evening after evening, in a strange city ... The restaurant was Greek, cosy, comfortable, and for the neighbourhood. The food was cheap, tasty and filling.

Over white beans with chopped onions, veal cutlet with a savoury dressing, and eventually a fruit cobbler and coffee, I read the *De Ethica* in its Everyman edition, Draftech pen at the ready to underline passages I might want to refind easily, later. Soul and mind were being fed together. I have not eaten alone in a restaurant in many years, but I see others doing it, and envy them.

Guy Davenport, 'On reading' (1987).

If the reading of good books is ever sinful, it is at meal-times. He who reads at meal-times treats his meal and his digestion with discourtesy, and puts upon his author the affront of a divided allegiance.

Robert Blatchford, *My Favourite Books* (1900).

* * * * *

I dislike a grand library to study in. I mean an immense apartment, with books all in Museum order, especially wire-safed. I say nothing against the Museum itself, or public libraries. They are capital places to go to, but not to sit in; and talking of this, I hate to read in public, and in strange company. The jealous silence; the dissatisfied looks of the messengers; the inability to help yourself; the not knowing whether you really ought to trouble the messengers, much less the Gentleman in black, or brown, who is, perhaps, half a trustee; with a variety of other jarrings between privacy and publicity.

Leigh Hunt, 'My books' (1823).

For myself, public libraries possess a special horror, as of lonely wastes and dragon-haunted fens. The stillness and the heavy air, the feeling of restriction and surveillance, the mute presence of these other readers, 'all silent and damned', combine to set up a nervous irritation fatal to quiet study.

Kenneth Grahame, 'Non libri sed liberi' (1894).

* * * * *

I can remember when I read any book, as the act of reading adheres to the room, the chair, the season. Doughty's *Arabia Deserta* I read under the hundred-year-old fig-tree in our backyard in South Carolina, a summer vacation from teaching at Washington University, having lucked onto the two volumes (minus the map that ought to have been in a pocket in vol. II) at a St Louis rummage sale.

Guy Davenport, 'On reading' (1987).

I am not much a friend to out-of-doors reading. I cannot settle my spirits to it. I knew a Unitarian minister, who was generally to be seen upon Snow-hill, between the hours of ten and eleven in the morning, studying a volume of Lardner. I owe this to have been a strain of abstraction beyond my reach. I used to admire how he sidled along, keeping clear of secular contacts. An illiterate encounter with a porter's knot, or a bread basket, would have quickly put to flight all the theology I am master of . . .

Charles Lamb, 'Detached thoughts on books and reading' (1833).

The only exercise in which he can be said to have excelled was that of threading crowded streets with his eyes fixed upon a book. He might be seen in such thoroughfares as Oxford Street, and Cheapside, walking as fast as other people walked, and reading a great deal faster than anybody else could read.

George Trevelyan, *The Life and Letters of Lord Macaulay* (1876).

Give me Books, fruit, French wine and fine weather and a little music out of doors, played by somebody I do not know.

John Keats, letter to Fanny Keats, 28 August, 1819.

*****

No apparatus, no appointment of time and place, is necessary for the enjoyment of reading.

John Aikin, *Letters from a Father to a Son* (1795).

4. 'CATALOGUED, AND RANGED UPON THE BOOK-SHELVES': BOOKNESTING

Movables of every kind lay strewn about, without the least attempt at order, and were intermixed with boxes, hampers, and all sorts of lumber. On all the floors were piles of books, to the amount, perhaps, of some thousands of volumes; these, still in bales: those, wrapped in paper, as they had been purchased: others scattered singly or in heaps: not one upon the shelves which lined the walls. To these Mr Fips called Tom's attention.

'Before anything else can be done, we must have them put in order, catalogued, and ranged upon the book-shelves, Mr Pinch. That will do to begin with, I think, sir.'

Tom rubbed his hands in the pleasant anticipation of a task so congenial to his taste.

Charles Dickens, *Martin Chuzzlewit* (1843–4).

There were three shelves of books in the house where I was born, on the dining-room wall between the fireplace and the wireless set. My parents moved into the house after their marriage and left it sixty-five years later when they died. During that time the books changed very little, though my father disposed of some of his physics books after Hiroshima.

Jane Gardam, in *The Pleasure of Reading* (1992).

Sitting, last winter, among my books, and walled round with all the comfort and protection which they and my fireside could afford me; to wit, a table of high-piled books at my back, my writing-desk on one side of me, some shelves on the other, and the feeling of the warm fire at my feet; I began to consider how I loved the authors of those books: how I loved them, too, not only for the imaginative pleasures they afforded me, but for their making me love the very books themselves, and delight to be in contact with them.

Leigh Hunt, 'My books' (1823).

His papers and his books rose in jagged mounds on table and floor, round which he skirted with nervous care lest his dressing-gown might disarrange them ever so slightly. On a chair stood a stack of photographs of statues and pictures, which it was his habit to exhibit, one by one, for the space of a day or two. The books on his shelves were as orderly as regiments of soldiers, and the backs of them shone like so many bronze beetle-wings; though, if you took one from its place you saw a shabbier volume behind it, since space was limited.

Virginia Woolf, *Night and Day* (1919).

. . . there are some publishers whom I refuse to collect, because all their novels look alike, and destroy my conception of a book-shelf, which should be a mass of gaudy variety.

Cyril Connolly, 'The novel-addict's cupboard' (1945).

The wall opposite the sunny window is tiled with the spines of some 1,600 battered paperbacks. They are umber, grey, brown and blue, they are as pleasingly textured and involving to the eye as the robes of the couple in Klimt's *The Kiss*, a reproduction of which hangs on the wall opposite me. Their battered backs are a mnemonic of my own history. Despite the gearing of my own book collection into that of my wife, this impression has been enhanced, rather than diminished. It must be because we are both the same kind of trampish bibliophagists. Unlike other, more fastidious types, our collecting instinct is akin to the spirit in which homeless people acquire shopping trolleys, then use them to mass everything the verge, the bin and the gutter have to offer, creating small mobile monuments to obsolescence.

Thus we have all the books no one else wanted – as well as most of the ones we did. That's why we have Tony Buzan's *Memory: How to Improve It*, as well as *Extracts from Gramsci's Prison Notebooks*; that's why there are all of my dead mother's Viragos, and the family Penguins, Pelicans and Puffins, paperback generics which have come together in chunks, after generation upon generation of packing them into cardboard boxes, resulting in the evolution of a crude librarianism. But only very crude. J. K. Galbraith still abuts C. S. Lewis abutting Arthur C. Clarke, who in turn leans on *Zen Comics* and a collection of *Helpful Hints* compiled by some upper-class supernumerary. Good cladding – and an entirely suitable housing within which to stay firmly at home.

Will Self, *Granty 65* (1999).

There was one comfort that, if he died, he would die in the midst of his books. There they were in the big bookcase, snug in a recess to the side of the fireplace. Marshalled tightly together, there they were, the books he used to read, pore, and ponder over: a regiment of theological controversial books, officered by d'Aubigné's *History of the Reformation*, Milner's *End of Controversy*, Chillingworth's *Protestantism*, holding forth that the Bible, and the Bible alone, is the religion of protestants, with an engraving of the fat face of the old cod stuck in the front of it; Foxe's *Book of Martyrs*, full of fire and blood and brimstone, *Popery Practical Paganism, Was St Peter Ever in Rome?* having in it a picture of divines battering each other with books, and SS. Peter and Paul, in the clouds of heaven, looking down and laughing at the fighters, actually saying, if pictures could speak, Go it, boys, give each other socks. Like inspection officers, the English Bible, the Latin Vulgate, and the Douai Testament stood pompously together,

and, to the right, *Cruden's Concordance* acting as orderly
officer; a neatly uniformed company of Dickens', Scott's,
George Eliot's, Meredith's, and Thackeray's novels; Shakespeare's Works; Burns', Keats', Milton's, Gray's, and Pope's
poetry; on the top shelf, six or seven huge volumes, like podgy
generals, of *The Decline and Fall of the Roman Empire*; and
leaning idly by their side was Locke's *Essay on the Human
Understanding*; and a whole crowd of school books that had
been used by the boys and Ella, with a number of camp fol-
lowers consisting of prizes they had won at Sunday school,
such as *I and Jesus with the Zulus*; *Little Crowns and How to
Win Them*; *Boys and Girls of the Bible*; *Gospel Garlands for
Little Girls*; *The Sieges of Gibraltar*; *From Crécy to Tel-el
Kebir*; while in the corner was a shy little book calling itself
Creation's Testimony to God; and locked away in a drawer,
forbidden to be touched by anyone save the head of the
house, lay a mysterious book which the father said confined
the dangerous teaching of a Bishop Berkeley; and, mother
added, was all about nothing being real, and that all things
we saw were only images of our own ideas, and that such
books were only to be read and thought of by minds big
enough to understand that they were rubbish.

Sean O'Casey, *I Knock at the Door* (1939).

* * * * *

There are books which I love to see on the shelf. I feel that
virtue goes out of them, but I should think it undue familiarity to read them.

Samuel McChord Crothers, *The Gentle Reader* (1903).

Of course, you know there are many fine houses where the
library is part of the upholstery, so to speak. Books in handsome binding kept locked under plate-glass in showy dwarf

book-cases are as important to stylish establishments as servants in livery, who sit with folded arms, are to stylish
equipages. I suppose those wonderful statues with the folded
arms do sometimes change their attitude, and I suppose those
books with the gilded backs do sometimes get opened, but it
is nobody's business whether they do or not, and it is not best
to ask too many questions.

Oliver Wendell Holmes, *The Poet at the Breakfast Table* (1872).

I lived in that apartment with over a thousand books. They
had originally belonged to my Uncle Victor, and he had collected them slowly over the course of about thirty years. Just
before I went off to college, he impulsively offered them to me
as a going-away present. I did my best to refuse, but Uncle
Victor was a sentimental and generous man, and would not
let me turn him down. 'I have no money to give you,' he said,
'and not one word of advice. Take the books to make me
happy.' I took the books, but for the next year and a half I did
not open any of the boxes they were stored in. My plan was to
persuade my uncle to take the books back, and in the meantime I did not want anything to happen to them.

As it turned out, the boxes were quite useful to me in that
state. The apartment on 112th Street was unfurnished, and
rather than squander my funds on things I did not want and
could not afford, I converted the boxes into several pieces of
'imaginary furniture.' It was a little like working on a puzzle:
grouping the cartons into various modular configurations,
lining them up in rows, stacking them one on top of another,
arranging and re-arranging them until they finally began to
resemble household objects. One set of sixteen served as the
support for my mattress, another set of twelve became a
table, others of seven became chairs, another of two became a
bedstand, and so on. The overall effect was rather monochro-
matic, what with that sombre light brown everywhere you

looked, but I could not help feeling proud of my resourceful-
ness. My friends found it a bit odd, but they had learned to
expect odd things from me by then. Think of the satisfaction,
I would explain to them, of crawling into bed and knowing
that your dreams are about to take place on top of nine-
teenth-century American literature. Imagine the pleasure of
sitting down to a meal with the entire Renaissance lurking
below your food. In point of fact, I had no idea which books
were in which boxes, but I was a great one for making up
stories back then, and I liked the sound of those sentences,
even if they were false.

Paul Auster, *Moon Palace* (1990).

The will-power necessary to get rid of books must be main-
tained at all costs. Even if one buys on a modest scale – say,
one book a day on an average – they fill room after room with
the inevitability of the rising tide. I once visited a house in
Blackheath after its owner had died. It was solid books.
Shelves had been abandoned years before; in every room
narrow lanes ran between books stacked from floor to ceiling,
ninety per cent of them utterly inaccessible. In one of the bed-
rooms there was a narrow space two feet wide round the bed,
and there the owner had died, almost entombed in print. This
macabre glimpse of the ultimate excesses of bibliomania has
always been a warning.

A. N. L. Munby, 'Floreat bibliomania' (1952).

*****

If one happened to be a person who never desired to refer
to his books the obvious thing to do would be to put the large
books into the large shelves and the small ones into the small
shelves and then go and smoke a self-satisfied pipe against the
nearest post. But to a man who prefers to know where every

book is, and who possesses, moreover, a sense of System and wishes everything to be in surroundings proper to its own qualities, this is not possible. Even an unsystematic man must choose to add a classification by subject to the compulsory classification by size; and, in my case, there is an added difficulty produced by a strong hankering for some sort of chronological order. There is nothing like that for easy reference. If you know that Beowulf will be at the left-hand end of the shelf that he fits and Julia Ward, the Sweet Singer of Michigan, at the right-hand end, you save yourself a good deal of time. But when your new compartments do not fit your old sections, when the large books of Stodge are so numerous as to insist upon intruding into the shelves reserved for large books of Pure Literature, and the duodecimos of Foreign Verse surge in a tidal wave over the preserves of the small books on Free Trade, Ethics, and Paleontology, one is reduced to the verge of despair. That is where I am at this moment; sitting in the midst of a large floor covered with sawdust, white distemper, nails, tobacco-ash, burnt matches, and the Greatest Works of the World's Greatest Masters. Fortunately, in Ruskin's words, 'I don't suppose I shall do it again for months and months and months.'

J. C. Squire, 'Moving a library' (1927).

Both in my library at home and in my bookshops I have a hard time hewing to any strict philosophy of shelving. Shelving by chronology (Susan Sontag's method) doesn't always work for me. The modest Everyman edition of *The Anglo Saxon Chronicle* refuses to sit comfortably next to Leonard Baskin's tall *Beowulf*, and exactly the same problem – incompatibility of size – crops up if one shelves alphabetically. Susan Sontag, on a visit when all my books were in the old ranch house, found that she couldn't live even one night with the sloppiness of my shelving. She imposed a hasty chronologizing which held for some years and still holds, in the main.

Susan's principles notwithstanding, I make free with chronologies when the books seem to demand it. My Sterne looks happier beside my Defoe than he looks next to his nearer contemporary Smollett, so *Tristram Shandy* sits next to *Moll Flanders* rather than *Peregrine Pickle.*

Despite a nearly infinite range of possibilities in the matter of book arrangement, I've noticed that most people who really love books find ways of shelving them which respect the books but clearly reflect their own personalities. The historian and scholar Robert Manson Myres had the most impeccably shelved library I have ever seen; he even had an alcove shelved in his Georgian apartment in Washington which held, precisely, his one-thousand-volume collection of the Everyman Library. The polymath Huntington Cairns, who had sixteen thousand books in a vast, smoky old apartment, in the same city, held to a rough subject arrangement, with no attempt being made to organize the books within a subject. He had 750 volumes on Plato and Aristotle alone, but was confident that, among them, he could find the book he needed when he required it.

Larry McMurtry, *Walter Benjamin at the Dairy Queen* (1999).

Our first work in settling here was to place upon new shelves the books which I had collected round myself at Waltham. And this work, which was in itself great, entailed also the labour of a new catalogue. As all who use libraries know, a catalogue is nothing unless it show the spot on which every book is to be found, – information which every volume also ought to give as to itself. Only those who have done it know how great is the labour of moving and arranging a few thousand volumes.

Anthony Trollope, *An Autobiography* (1883).

I do not remember that any of our meditative essayists has written on the subject of Moving One's Books. If such an essay exists I should be glad to go to it for sympathy and consolation. . . . Night after night I have spent carting down two flights of stairs more books than I ever thought I possessed. Journey after journey, as monotonously regular as the progresses of a train round the Inner Circle: upstairs empty handed, and downstairs creeping with a decrepit crouch, a tall, crazy, dangerously bulging column of books wedged between my two hands and the indomitable point of my chin. The job simply has to be done; once it is started there is no escape from it; but at times during the process one hates books as the slaves who built the pyramids must have hated public monuments. A strong and bitter book-sickness floods one's soul. How ignominious to be strapped to this ponderous mass of paper, print, and dead men's sentiments! Would it not be better, finer, braver, to leave the rubbish where it lies and walk out into the world a free, untrammelled, illiterate Superman? Civilization! Pah! But that mood is, I'm happy to say, with me ephemeral. It is generated by the necessity for tedious physical exertion and dies with the need. Nevertheless the actual transport is about the briefest and least harassing of the operations called for. Dusting (or 'buffeting the books' as Dr Johnson called it) is a matter of choice. One can easily say to oneself, 'These books were banged six months ago' (knowing full well that it was really twelve months ago), and thus decide to postpone the ceremony until everything else has been settled. But the complications of getting one's library straight are still appalling.

J. C. Squire, 'Moving a library' (1927).

On Wednesday, April 3, in the morning I found him very busy putting his books in order, and as they were generally very old ones, clouds of dust were flying around him. He had on a pair of large gloves, such as hedgers use. His present appearance put me in mind of my uncle, Dr Boswell's description of him, 'A robust genius, born to grapple with whole libraries.'

James Boswell, *Life of Johnson* (1791).

I believe it then to be quite simply true that books have their own very personal feeling about their place on the shelves. They like to be close to suitable companions, and I remember once on coming into my library that I was persistently disturbed by my 'Jane Eyre'. Going up to it, wondering what was the matter with it, restless because of it, I only after a morning's uneasiness discovered that it had been placed next to my Jane Austens, and anyone who remembers how sharply Charlotte criticised Jane will understand why this would never do.

Hugh Walpole, *These Diversions: Reading* (1926).

Conscious of my propriety and comfort in these matters, I take an interest in the bookcases as well as the books of my friends. I long to meddle, and dispose them after my own notions.

Leigh Hunt, 'My books' (1823).

Some friends of *theirs* had rented their house for several months to an interior decorator. When they returned, they discovered that their entire library had been reorganized by color and size. Shortly thereafter, the decorator met with a fatal automobile accident. I confess that when this story was told, everyone around the dinner table concurred that justice had been served.

Anne Fadiman, *Ex Libris: Confessions of a Common Reader* (1998).

I had a very small library at this time, but my fine poets and dramatists, my superior essayists and one or two French novels (the last almost entirely unintelligible to me) were arranged ostentatiously upon my shelves; I was always vexed did anyone come into my room and not notice them.

Hugh Walpole, *These Diversions: Reading* (1926).

I keep novels and detective stories in my bedroom, so that visitors shan't be tempted to borrow them; the sitting-room houses the higher forms of literature (and my jazz books, a far from exhaustive collection), while the hall I reserve for thoroughly worthy items, to speed the parting guest.

Philip Larkin, 'Books' (1972).

*****

. . . there was nothing that would lighten the burden of gloom. Except, I hoped, the hospital library. But the library was a remnant of the puritanical Stalinist era, and it contained only three kinds of books: long rows of Collected Works by diverse Soviet and Czechoslovak statesmen (unopened); volumes of early Czech socialist realism (opened occasionally, and quickly shut); and finally Czech and Russian classics. I borrowed a copy of *Selected Shorter Works by L. N. Tolstoy* and, guided by Murphy's Law, opened it on a page which gave a detailed description of the last hours in the life of Ivan Ilyich. That put an end to my appetite for reading classics in the hospital, and I sent out word to friends to provide me with privately owned books.

Josef Škvorecký, 'The pleasures of the freedom to read' (1987).

She was generous with her books, too – eventually shelving them in every room of the bleak infirmary annex. But they outgrew the shelf space and slid into the main infirmary, into the waiting room, and into X-ray, first covering and then replacing the newspapers and the magazines. Slowly, the sick of the Steering School learned what a serious place Steering was – not your ordinary hospital, crammed with light reading and the media trash. While you were waiting to see the doctor, you could browse through *The Waning of the Middle Ages*; waiting for your lab results, you could ask the nurse to bring you that invaluable genetics manual, *The Fruit Fly Handbook*. If you were seriously ill, or might be visiting the infirmary for a long time, there was sure to be a copy of *The Magic Mountain*. For the boy with the broken leg, and all the athletically wounded, there were the good heroes and their meaty adventures – there were Conrad and Melville instead of *Sport Illustrated*; instead of *Time* and *Newsweek*, there were Dickens and Hemingway and Twain. What a wet dream for the lovers of literature, to lie sick at Steering! At last, a hospital with something good to read.

When Jenny Fields had spent twelve years at Steering, it was a habit among the school librarians, upon recognizing that they didn't have a book which someone sought, to say, 'Perhaps the infirmary has it.'

And at the bookstore, when someone was out of stock or out of print, they might recommend that you 'find Nurse Fields over at the infirmary; *she* might have it.'

And Jenny would frown upon hearing the request, and say, 'I believe that's in twenty-six, at the annex, but McCarty is reading it. He has the flu. Perhaps when he's through, he'll be glad to let you have it.' Or she might respond, 'I last saw that one down at the whirlpool bath. It might be a little wet, in the beginning.'

John Irving, *The World According to Garp* (1976).

*****

When at home, I a little more frequent my library from whence I at once survey all the whole concerns of my family. As I enter it, I from thence see under my garden, court, and base-court, and into all the parts of the building. There I turn over now one book, and then another, of various subjects, without method or design . . . The figure of my study is round, and has no more flat wall than what is taken up by my table and chair; so that the remaining parts of the circle present me a view of all my books at once, set upon five degrees of shelves round about me. It has three noble and free prospects, and is sixteen paces diameter.

Michel de Montaigne, 'Of three commerces' (1580).

The room was lit by a chandelier whose light, unable to reach the extremities of the room lit only the spines of those volumes on the central shelves of the long walls. A stone gallery ran round the library at about fifteen feet above the floor, and the books that lined the walls of the main hall fifteen feet below were continued upon the high shelves of the gallery.

In the middle of the room, immediately under the light, stood a long table. It was carved from a single piece of the blackest marble, which reflected upon its surface three of the rarest volumes in his Lordship's collection.

Upon his knees, drawn up together, was balanced a book of his grandfather's essays, but it had remained unopened. His arms lay limply at his side, and his head rested against the velvet of the chair back. He was dressed in the grey habit which it was his custom to wear in the library. From full sleeves his sensitive hands emerged with the shadowy transparency of alabaster. For an hour he had remained thus; the deepest melancholy manifested itself in every line of his body.

The library appeared to spread outwards from him as from a core. His dejection infected the air about him and diffused its illness upon every side. All things in the long room absorbed his melancholia. The shadowing galleries brooded with slow anguish; the books receding into the deep corners, tier upon tier, seemed each a separate tragic note in a monumental fugue of volumes.

Mervyn Peake, *Titus Groan* (1946).

His library was situated on the fourth and topmost floor of No. 24 Ehrlich Strasse. The door of the flat was secured by three highly complicated locks. He unlocked them, strode across the hall, which contained nothing except an umbrella and coat-stand, and entered his study. Carefully he set down the briefcase on an armchair. Then once and again he paced the entire length of the four lofty, spacious communicating rooms which formed his library. The entire wall-space up to the ceiling was clothed with books. Slowly he lifted his eyes towards them. Skylights had been let into the ceiling. He was proud of his roof-lighting. The windows had been walled up several years before after a determined struggle with his landlord. In this way he had gained in every room a fourth wall-space; accommodation for more books. Moreover illumination from above, which lit up all the shelves equally, seemed to him more just and more suited to his relations with his books. The temptation to watch what went on in the street – an immoral and time-wasting habit – disappeared with the side windows. Daily, before he sat down to his writing desk, he blessed both the idea and its results, since he owed to them the fulfilment of his dearest wish: the possession of a well-stocked library, in perfect order and enclosed on all sides, in which no single superfluous article of furniture, no single superfluous person could lure him from his serious thoughts.

The first of the four rooms served for his study. A huge old writing desk, an armchair in front of it, a second armchair in the opposite corner were its only furniture. There crouched besides an unobtrusive divan, willingly overlooked by its master: he only slept on it. A movable pair of steps was propped against the wall. It was more important than the divan, and travelled in the course of a day from room to room. The emptiness of the three remaining rooms was not disturbed by so much as a chair. Nowhere did a table, a cupboard, a fireplace interrupt the multi-coloured monotony of the bookshelves. Handsome deep-pile carpets, the uniform covering of the floor, softened the harsh twilight which, mingling through wide-open communicating doors, made of the four separate rooms one single lofty hall.

Elias Canetti, *Auto da Fé* (1935).

. . . but for the study itself, give me a small snug place, almost entirely walled with books. There should be only one window in it, looking upon trees.

Leigh Hunt, 'My books' (1823).

5. LEAVING TO ONE SIDE 'FRIVOLITIES LIKE READING': BOOKISH BEHAVIOUR

I began my life as I shall no doubt end it: among books. In my grandfather's study, they were everywhere; it was forbidden to dust them except once a year, before the October term. Even before I could read, I already revered these raised stones; upright or leaning, wedged together like bricks on the library shelves or nobly spaced like avenues of dolmens, I felt that our family prosperity depended on them. They were all alike, and I was romping about in a tiny sanctuary, surrounded by squat, ancient monuments which had witnessed my birth, which would witness my death and whose permanence guaranteed me a future as calm as my past. I used to touch them in secret to honour my hands with their dust but I did not have much idea what to do with them and each day I was present at ceremonies whose meaning escaped me: my grandfather – so clumsy, normally, that my grandmother buttoned his gloves for him – handled these cultural objects with the dexterity of an officiating priest. Hundreds of times I saw him get up absent-mindedly, walk round the table, cross the room in two strides, unhesitatingly pick out a volume without allowing himself time for choice, run through it as he went back to his armchair, with a combined movement of his thumb and right forefinger, and, almost before he sat down, open it with a flick 'at the right page', making it creak like a shoe. I sometimes got close enough to observe these boxes which opened like oysters and I discovered the nakedness of their internal organs, pale, dank, slightly blistered pages, covered with small black veins, which drank ink and smelt of mildew.

Jean-Paul Sartre, *Words* (1964).

The best bookcase moment, I find, is when you reach up to get a paperback that happens to sit on one of the higher shelves, above your head. You single it out by putting a fingertip atop the block of its pages and pulling gently down, so that the book rocks forward and a triangle of cover design appears from between the paperbacks on either side. The book's emergence is steadied and slowed by the mild lateral pressure of its shelved peers, and, if you stop pulling just then, it will hang there by itself, at an angle, leaning out over the room like an admonishing piece of architectural detail; it will not fall. Finally the moment of equilibrium passes: the book's displaced centre of gravity and the narrowing area it has available for adjacent friction conspire to release its weight to you, and it drops forward into your open hand. You catch the book that you chose to make fall.

Nicholson Baker, 'Books as furniture' (1995).

I could see as well as he did that although peasants did not like new books, they treated them with respect, touched them carefully, half-expecting them to fly away at any moment like a bird from their hands. I loved to see them do this, since for me books were indeed something wonderful.

Maxim Gorky, *My Apprenticeship* (1915).

He oozes intelligence from every pore: a restless, inquisitive rationalist. You realise, watching this performance, that Hamlet the perceptive, thoughtful, relentlessly inquiring man, the practical diplomat and courtier, is far more essential to the reading of the play than Hamlet the professional intellectual. Of course he is cultivated and refined: when he picks up Ophelia's book from the floor for her, he glances at it to see what it is, like anyone to whom books are vital nourishment.

J. Peter, reviewing Ian Charleson's *Hamlet*, *The Sunday Times*, 12 November, 1989.

* * * * *

Her eyes explored everything – the Beidermeier furniture, the piano, the old grandfather clock, the pictures, the bookcases, the plates and cutlery on the table. When I left her alone to prepare pudding, she was not at the table when I came back. She had gone from room to room and was standing in my father's study. I leaned quietly against the doorpost and watched her. She let her eyes drift over the bookshelves that filled the walls, as if she were reading a text. Then she went to a shelf, raised her right index finger chest high and ran it slowly along the backs of the books, moved to the next shelf, ran her finger further along, from one spine to the next, pacing off the whole room. She stopped at the window, looked out into the darkness, at the reflection of the bookshelves, and at her own.

Bernhard Schlink, The Reader (1997).

There is also that kind of reading which is just looking at books. From time to time – I can't say what dictates the impulse – I pull a chair up in front of a section of my library. An expectant tranquillity settles over me. I move my eyes slowly, reading the spines, or identifying the title by its colour and positioning. Just to see my books, to note their presence, their proximity to other books, fills me with a sense of futurity.

Sven Birkerts, 'Notes from a confession' (1987).

'I suppose you read your books?' ask cynical friends from time to time, wrenching from its shelf and brusquely opening some book which they know perfectly well to be unreadable, such as the Aldine *Odyssey* on vellum, printed in an intricately contracted Greek type, or Frederick the Great's copy of a fifth-rate Roman historian. This is what the Latin grammars call a question-expecting-the-answer-no, and I do not disappoint their expectation. Reading them, I explain, is hardly necessary. Any don will agree that in some occult manner knowledge can be imbibed merely by sitting with half-closed eyes in a room lined with books. In fact I do read them and I constantly lend books to other people who I think would read them with greater profit than myself. For the most part however I just look at them or take them down and stroke them from time to time. Book-collecting, I would have you know, is a full-time occupation, and one wouldn't get far if one took time off for frivolities like reading.

A. N. L. Munby, 'Floreat bibliomania' (1952).

When I speak of being in contact with my books, I mean it literally. I like to lean my head against them.

Leigh Hunt, 'My books' (1823).

* * * * *

Observational studies conducted during the past four years at the University of Tennessee establish that adult book-carrying behaviour is sexually dimorphic. Most males carry books at their sides with their arms relatively straight while women usually rest the books on their hips or pelvic bones and cradle them with their arms. It appears that employing appropriate sex-typed book-carrying styles is important for peer acceptance.

T. Hanaway and G. Burghardt, 'The development of sexually dimorphic book-carrying behaviour' (1976).

Among the proprietors of smaller shops there were one or two early risers, who might be seen busying themselves behind their open doors from half past seven onwards. Defying these temptations, Kien tapped his own well-filled briefcase. He clasped it tightly to him, in a very particular manner which he had himself thought out, so that the greatest possible area of his body was always in contact with it. Even his ribs could feel its presence through his cheap, thin suit. His upper arm covered the whole side elevation; it fitted exactly. The lower portion of his arm supported the case from below. His outstretched fingers splayed out over every part of the flat surface to which they yearned. He privately excused himself for this exaggerated care because of the value of the contents. Should the briefcase by any mischance fall to the ground, or should the lock, which he tested every morning before setting out, spring open at precisely that perilous moment, ruin would come to his priceless volumes. There was nothing he loathed more intensely than battered books.

Elias Canetti, *Auto da Fé* (1935).

* * * * *

Rose early, and finding Lamb bent on going away made up a fire and breakfast for him and accompanied him to the Enfield stage, loading him with books, a print of Blake's Chaucer's Pilgrims and a bottle of shrub.

Henry Crabb Robinson, diary entry for 22 May, 1828.

His avidity as a reader – his desire to master his subject – led to some charming eccentricities, as when, for a daily journey between Earl's Court Road and Addison Road stations, he would carry a heavy hand-bag filled with books, 'to read in the train'. This was no satire on the railway system, but pure zeal.

E. V. Lucas, 'A funeral' (1907).

All tourists cherish an illusion, of which no amount of experience can ever completely cure them; they imagine that they will find time, in the course of their travels, to do a lot of reading. They see themselves, at the end of a day's sight-seeing or motoring, or while they are sitting in the train, studiously turning over the pages of all the vast and serious works which, at ordinary seasons, they never find time to read. They start for a fortnight's tour in France, taking with them *The Critique of Pure Reason, Appearance and Reality*, the complete works of Dante, and the *Golden Bough*. They come home to make the discovery that they have read something less than half a chapter of the *Golden Bough* and the first fifty-two lines of the *Inferno*. But that does not prevent them from taking just as many books the next time they set out on their travels.

Long experience has taught me to reduce in some slight measure the dimension of my travelling library. But even now I am far too optimistic about my powers of reading while on a journey. Along with the books which I know it is possible to read, I still continue to put in a few impossible volumes in the pious hope that some day, somehow, they will get read. Thick tomes have travelled with me for thousands of kilometres across the face of Europe and have returned with their secrets unviolated.

Aldous Huxley, 'Books for the journey' (1925).

Anita Brookner and I are going on holiday together to St Andrews. A couple of years back I went with George Eliot to Raasay but it was not a barrel of laughs; there's still a book-mark in my disintegrating Penguin copy of *Daniel Deronda* at page 289, in the middle of the chapter called 'Maidens Choosing', signposting where we parted company.

A. Taylor, *The List*, 22–29 August, 1988.

I took it [*Gravity's Rainbow*] on holiday to Greece with me in 1987. For three days I manfully ploughed on until I realised that it was actually ruining my vacation. I'd only got to page 127, and in the meantime my friend had not only polished off *Kennedy for the Defence* but was steaming through *A House for Mr Biswas*. I jettisoned it in the left luggage locker at Nafplio station. It's probably still there.

'I like to read', *The Guardian*, 29 May, 2004.

After dinner we talked a little more, Featherstone put on the gramophone, and we looked at the latest illustrated papers that had arrived from England. Then we went to bed. Featherstone came to my room to see that I had everything I wanted.

'I suppose you haven't any books with you,' he said. 'I haven't got a thing to read.'

'Books?' I cried.

I pointed to my book-bag. It stood upright, bulging oddly, so that it looked like a humpbacked gnome somewhat the worse for liquor.

'Have you got books in there? I thought that was your dirty linen or a camp-bed or something. Is there anything you can lend me?'

'Look for yourself.'

Featherstone's boys had unlocked the bag, but quailing before the sight that then discovered itself had done no more. I knew from long experience how to unpack it. I threw it over on its side, seized its leather bottom and, walking backwards, dragged the sack away from its contents. A river of books poured on to the floor. A look of stupefaction came upon Featherstone's face.

'You don't mean to say you travel with as many books as that? By George, what a snip!'

He bent down and turning them over rapidly looked at the

titles. There were books of all kinds. Volumes of verse, novels, philosophical works, critical studies (they say books about books are profitless, but they certainly make very pleasant reading), biographies, histories; there were books to read when you were ill and books to read when your brain, all alert, craved for something to grapple with; there were books that you had always wanted to read, but in the hurry of life at home had never found time to; there were books to read at sea when you were meandering through narrow waters on a tramp steamer, and there were books for bad weather when your whole cabin creaked and you had to wedge yourself in your bunk in order not to fall out; there were books chosen solely for their length, which you took with you when on some expedition you had to travel light, and there were books you could read when you could read nothing else.

W. Somerset Maugham, 'The book bag' (1951).

A cousin of mine from Buenos Aires was deeply aware that books could function as a badge, a sign of alliance, and always chose a book to take on her travels with the same care with which she chose her handbag. She would not travel with Romain Rolland because she thought it made her look too pretentious, or with Agatha Christie because it made her look too vulgar. Camus was appropriate for a short trip, Cronin for a long one; a detective story by Vera Caspary or Ellery Queen was acceptable for a weekend in the country; a Graham Greene novel was suitable for travelling by ship or plane.

Alberto Manguel, *A History of Reading* (1996).

It's probable that you've also (smugly) noticed 'inverse literary air-class syndrome', first observed by Martin Amis. In Economy, earnest students are grappling with the *Epic of Gilgamesh* or *The Brothers Karamazov* while calculating how

many complimentary mini-bags of pretzels they can reasonably demand from the stewardess. Meanwhile in Club a few
brave souls are struggling with John Grisham, or even, dar-
ingly, *Stupid White Men*. Then step through to First where the
jaded businessman is idly leafing through *High Life*, or with a
confused expression on his careworn features, scrutinising
the duty-free leaflet.

'I like to read', *The Guardian*, 29 May, 2004.

In the pocket of my coat was *The Prelude*, the only book I
had brought. I brought it because I know of no other book
that is at the same time so slender and so satisfying. It slips
even into a woman's pocket, and has an extraordinarily filling
effect on the mind. Its green limp covers are quite worn with
the journeys it has been with me. I take it everywhere I go;
and I have read it and read it for many summers without yet
having entirely assimilated its adorable stodginess.

Elizabeth von Arnim, *The Adventures of Elizabeth in Rugen* (1904).

'You shouldn't,' said Davey, 'read in trains, ever. It's madly
wearing to the optic nerve centres, it imposes a most fearful
strain.'

Nancy Mitford, *The Pursuit of Love* (1945).

*****

Nor can I throw a book away. I have given many away and
ripped a few in half, but as with warring nations, destruction
shows regard: the enemy is a power to reckon with. Throwing
a book out shows contempt for an effort of the spirit. Not
that I haven't tried. Among some tossed-out books of my
daughter's which I rescued, to shelter until a foster home
could be arranged, was one too awful to live. I returned it to
the trash, resisting the urge to say a few parting words. All

day long the thought of its mingling with chicken bones and olive pits nagged me. Half a dozen times I removed it and replaced it, like an executioner with scruples about capital punishment. Finally I put it on a high shelf where I wouldn't have to see it. Life imprisonment.

Lynne Sharon Schwartz, *Ruined by Reading* (1996).

I houseclean my books every spring and throw out those I'm never going to read again like I throw out clothes I'm never going to wear again. It shocks everybody. My friends are peculiar about books. They read all the best sellers, they get through them as fast as possible, I think they skip a lot. And they NEVER read anything a second time so they don't remember a word of it a year later. But they are profoundly shocked to see me drop a book in the wastebasket or give it away. The way they look at it, you buy a book, you read it, you put it on the shelf, you never open it again for the rest of your life but YOU DON'T THROW IT OUT! NOT IF IT HAS A HARD COVER ON IT! Why not? I personally can't think of anything less sacrosanct than a bad book or even a mediocre book.

Helene Hanff, letter to Frank Doel, 18 September, 1952.

* * * * *

We talked books. We just simply enumerated books without end, praising or damning them, and arranged authors in neat pews, like cattle in classes at an agricultural show. No pastime is more agreeable to people who have the book disease, and none more quickly fleets the hours, and none is more delightfully futile.

Arnold Bennett, 'The death of Simon Fuge' (1907).

*****

Miss Bingley's attention was quite as much engaged in watching Mr Darcy's progress through *his* book, as in reading her own; and she was perpetually either making some inquiry, or looking at his page. She could not win him, however, to any conversation; he merely answered her question, and read on. At length, quite exhausted by the attempt to be amused with her own book, which she had only chosen because it was the second volume of his, she gave a great yawn and said, 'How pleasant it is to spend an evening in this way! I declare after all there is no enjoyment like reading! How much sooner one tires of anything than of a book! – When I have a house of my own, I shall be miserable if I have not an excellent library.'

Jane Austen, *Pride and Prejudice* (1813).

I do not remember a more whimsical surprise than having been once detected – by a familiar damsel – reclined at my ease upon the grass, on Primrose Hill, reading *Pamela*. There was nothing in the book to make a man seriously ashamed at the exposure; but as she seated herself down by me, and seemed determined to read in company, I could have wished it had been – any other book. We read on very sociably for a few pages; and, not finding the author much to her taste, she got up, and – went away. Gentle casuist, I leave it to thee to conjecture, whether the blush (for there was one between us) was the property of the nymph or the swain in this dilemma. From me you shall never get the secret.

Charles Lamb, 'Detached thoughts on books and reading' (1833).

*****

Wordsworth's habits of using books – which I am satisfied, would, in those days, alone have kept him at a distance from most men with fine libraries – were not vulgar; not the habits of those who turn over the page by means of a wet finger (though even this abomination I have seen perpetrated by a Cambridge tutor and fellow of a college; but then he had been bred up as a ploughman, and the son of a ploughman).

Thomas de Quincey, 'William Wordsworth and Robert Southey'

(1839).

. . . his bedside table currently supports three spreadeagled volumes. 'They are ready in an instant to let me pick them up,' he explains. 'To use an electronics analogy, closing a book on a bookmark is like pressing the Stop button, whereas when you leave the book facedown, you've only pressed Pause.'

Anne Fadiman, *Ex Libris: Confessions of a Common Reader* (1998).

6. 'AS RARE NOW AS GIANT PANDAS':
RAPACIOUS READERS

The world may be divided into people that read, people that write, people that think, and fox-hunters.

William Shenstone, 'On writing and books' (1769).

... I figured out that the way to find out what to read was to locate a great reader and follow in his or her tracks. There are, though, surprisingly few great readers – they are as rare now as giant pandas.

Larry McMurtry, *Walter Benjamin at the Dairy Queen* (1999).

*****

... in my early years I read very hard. It is a sad reflection, but a true one, that I knew almost as much at eighteen as I do now.

James Boswell, *Life of Johnson* (1791).

The paper drunkard reads all books, no matter what, so long as they are hard. He is not content with books that are being talked about; they have to be rare and forgotten, and hard to find. On occasion, he has been forced to spend a year hunting down a book because no one knew it. Once he finally has it, he reads it quickly, catches on, and can always quote from it. At seventeen, he looked the way he looks now at forty-seven. The more he reads, the more he stays the same. Any attempt to surprise him with a name goes awry; he is equally well-versed in every area. Since there is always something left that he does not yet know, he has never been bored.

But he makes sure never to let on what he does not know, so that no one else will read about it first.

> Elias Canetti, 'The paper drunkard' (1979).

His aim in life has been to get through as much printed matter as he possibly can without regard either to its fitness for him or his fitness for it. He has exercised his eyes at the expense of his brains. He prefers heavy works in many volumes, covering long periods with vast detail. He is a perfect arsenal of titles. His idea of rational conversation is to pin you in a corner and compare the number of books he has read with the number you have read, in the eager hope of making you ashamed of yourself.

> Austen Dobson, *A Bookman's Budget* (1917).

He put down *If I Were God*. 1884 and counting. Getting the books in the right order was impossible, and he couldn't be as neat as he'd like to be. He had to zigzag.

The Idea had come to him thirteen years ago on the third floor of the University Library, reading a letter by the extremely dead Pope Pius II: 'Without letters, every age is blind.' And he wondered what you would see if you had all the letters, if you had read everything ever written. He was already living in the library at that point, which was perhaps the start. . . .

He had never explained his mission to anyone, because he didn't want anyone to know if he failed, and because he wasn't sure what the point was. He sensed there was an answer at the end, but he had no idea what it would be or what he could do with it. Perhaps he would write something original. After all how can you write something original if you haven't read everything before?

The numbers are daunting. A few hundred books to 1500. Some ten thousand to 1600. Eighty thousand to 1700. Three hundred thousand to 1800. Then things go crazy. Much of it was recloaking. Much of it was dross. Much of it was brief. But if he hadn't come up with the two-book technique, simultaneously reading one book in his right hand and one book in his left, he wouldn't have got anywhere.

Tibor Fischer, 'Bookcruncher' (2001).

I need fiction. I'm an addict. This is not a figure of speech. I don't quite read a novel a day, but I certainly read some of a novel every day, and usually some of several. There is always a heap of opened paperbacks face down near the bed, always something current on the kitchen table to reach for over coffee when I wake up. Colonies of prose have formed in the bathroom and in the dimness of the upstairs landing, so that I don't go without text even in the leftover spaces of the house where I spend least time. When I'm tired and therefore indecisive, last thing at night, it can take half an hour to choose the book I am going to have with me while I brush my teeth.

Francis Spufford, *The Child that Books Built* (2002).

When *I* want a book, it is as a tiger wants a sheep. I must have it with one spring, and, if I miss it, go away defeated and hungry.

Oliver Wendell Holmes, *The Poet at the Breakfast Table* (1872).

This reading, for which I stole time from my work, became a new offence which brought new punishment upon me. The taste for it, provoked by constraint, became a passion, and soon a regular madness. La Tribu, a well-known lender of books, provided me with all kinds of literature. Good or bad, all were alike to me; I had no choice, and read everything with equal avidity. I read at the work-table, I read on my errands, I read in the wardrobe, and forgot myself for hours together, my head became giddy with reading; I could do nothing else. My master watched me,

surprised me, beat me, took away my books. How many
volumes were torn, burnt, and thrown out of the window!
how many works were left in odd volumes in La Tribu's
stock! when I had no more money to pay her, I gave her my
shirts, neckties and clothes; my three sous of pocket-money
were regularly taken to her every Sunday.

Jean-Jacques Rousseau, *The Confessions* (1781).

Deprived of their newspapers or a novel, reading-addicts
will fall back onto cookery books, on the literature which is
wrapped round bottles of patent medicine, on those instructions for keeping the contents crisp which are printed on the
outside of boxes of breakfast cereals. On anything.

Aldous Huxley, 'Writers and readers' (1936).

Any suggestion that my father's association with books was
governed by a developing strategy would be a wicked deceit.
Apart from my mother and his music, they were the light of
his life. They were his meat and drink. They were his bulwark
against the world. They became – it is impossible to deny – an
overpowering disease.

He bought them, read them, marked them, reread them,
stored them, reallocated them on the shelves, which spread
like erysipelas up every available wall, knew where each precious volume of the countless thousands nestled without the
aid of a catalogue. His appetite was gargantuan and insa-
tiable. He was a bibliophilial drunkard – with the difference
that the taste never palled and he never had a hangover. The
only stab of remorse he ever experienced was the rare recollection of how, at one of Hodgson's sales or in one of the
second-hand shops where he spent another of his lifetimes, a
temptation has been cravenly resisted. He would tell me over
lunch how he had been at the bookshop prompt at nine
o'clock that morning to repair some cowardly error of the

day before. The treasure was still there on the shelf. Who could want further proof of the intervention of Providence?

Since the house in Cornwall had still to be run as a place of human habitation my mother often found the pressure intolerable. So my father became furtive. He would get up early to waylay the postman or set off for London on a Monday morning with several empty suitcases. When he went on a lecture tour to America he returned with eleven cratefuls. When each member of the family was old enough to leave home, the parting could be borne. Valuable wall space was released. Wordsworth or Napoleon or Montaigne or Dr Johnson could at last have a room of his own, like John Milton.

> Michael Foot, 'Isaac Foot: A Rupert for the Roundheads' (1980).

There is a story of Auberon Herbert – I do not know whether it is true or not, but I do not mind connecting it with his name, because it is a story I think entirely to his credit, and which I always recall with a sense of satisfaction and encouragement. He was staying in his country home, and some visitors were announced. He received them with perfect good manners, and, after a cordial welcome, he said to them, 'And now what would you like to do? – we are reading.'

> Viscount Grey, 'The pleasure of reading' (1926).

An Oxford Cleric, still a student though,
One who had taken logic long ago,
Was there; his horse was thinner than a rake,
And he was not too fat, I undertake,
But had a hollow look, a sober stare;
The thread upon his overcoat was bare.
He had found no preferment in the church
And he was too unworldly to make search
For secular employment. By his bed

He preferred having twenty books in red
And black, of Aristotle's philosophy,
To having fine clothes, fiddle or psaltery.
Though a philosopher, as I have told,
He had not found the stone for making gold.
Whatever money from his friends he took
He spent on learning or another book
And prayed for them most earnestly, returning
Thanks to them thus for paying for his learning.
His only care was study, and indeed
He never spoke a word more than was need,
Formal at that, respectful in the extreme,
Short, to the point, and lofty in his theme.
The thought of moral virtue filled his speech
And he would gladly learn, and gladly teach.

Geoffrey Chaucer, *The Canterbury Tales* (*c.*1380s).

To the end he read books more quickly than other people skimmed them, and skimmed them as fast as anyone else could turn the leaves. 'He seemed to read through the skin,' said one who had often watched the operation. And this speed was not in his case obtained at the expense of accuracy. Anything which had once appeared in type, from the highest effort of genius down to the most detestable trash that ever consumed ink and paper manufactured for better things, had in his eyes an authority which led him to look upon misquotation as a species of minor sacrilege.

George Trevelyan, *The Life and Letters of Lord Macaulay* (1876).

'You read a lot,' said the behatted kvetch indicating the two novels he had open. He nodded, because there was no denying it and because he didn't want to put up the ante for a conversation.

'Books aren't life.'

'No, they're better,' he replied and flipped through the thirty-two library cards in his wallet to remove his one credit card to pay.

Tibor Fischer, 'Bookcruncher' (2001).

That was when I started reading Uncle Victor's books. Two weeks after the funeral, I picked out one of the boxes at random, slit the tape carefully with a knife, and read everything that was inside it. It proved to be a strange mixture, packed with no apparent order or purpose. There were novels and plays, history books and travel books, chess guides and detective stories, science fiction and works of philosophy – an absolute chaos of print. It made no difference to me. I read each book to the end and refused to pass judgement on it. As far as I was concerned, each book was equal to every other book, each sentence was composed of exactly the right number of words, and each word stood exactly where it had to be. That was how I chose to mourn my Uncle Victor. One by one, I would open every box, and one by one I would read every book. That was the task I set for myself, and I stuck with it to the bitter end.

Each box contained a jumble similar to the first, a hodge-podge of high and low, heaps of ephemera scattered among the classics, ragged paperbacks sandwiched between hard-bound editions, potboilers lying flush with Donne and Tolstoy. Uncle Victor had never organised his library in any systematic way. Each time he had bought a book, he had put it on the shelf next to the one he had bought before it, and little by little the rows had expanded, filling more and more space as the years went by. That was precisely how the books had entered the boxes. If nothing else, the chronology was intact, the sequence had been preserved by default. I considered this to be the ideal arrangement. Each time I opened a box, I was able to enter another segment of my uncle's life, a fixed period of days or weeks or months, and it consoled me to feel that I was occupying the same mental space that Victor had once occupied – reading the same words, living in the same stories, perhaps thinking the same thoughts.

Paul Auster, *Moon Palace* (1990).

* * * * *

That I can read and be happy while I am reading, is a great blessing. Could I have remembered, as some men do, what I read, I should have been able to call myself an educated man. But that power I have never possessed. Something is always left, – something dim and inaccurate, – but still something sufficient to preserve the taste for more. I am inclined to think that it is so with most readers.

Anthony Trollope, *An Autobiography* (1883).

There have indeed been minds overlaid by much reading, men who have piled such a load of books on their heads, their brains seemed to be squashed by them.

A. W. and J. C. Hare, *Guesses at Truth* (1827).

Hence it is, that he who reads very much and almost the whole day, amusing himself in the intervals of his reading with thoughtless pastime, gradually loses the capacity even to think, just as one who always rides at last forgets how to walk. But such is the case with many scholars; they have read themselves stupid.

Arthur Schopenhauer, 'On reading and books' (1851).

7. 'NOT SQUANDERING INCOME BUT SINKING CAPITAL': BUYING BOOKS

> The moment when one meets a book and knows, beyond shadow of doubt, that that book must be his – not necessarily now, but some time – is among the happiest excitements of the spirit.
>
> Christopher Morley, 'On visiting bookshops' (1925).

We lived at that time in an old dusty, crooked town whose streets were for ever going uphill; I was left a great deal to my own devices, and having on one occasion just before Christmas a penny to spend I determined to buy a book. I had never independently of my own account bought a book before; I didn't think it would be difficult to buy a book for a penny; a penny seemed to me a good deal of money. I went into the shop and asked what book I might have for a penny. The bookseller smiled and put in front of me a pile of thin little books bound in yellow paper. I can smell still the odd scent of those books, something musty like straw and pungent like cheese. I looked at them one after another and said that what I wanted was a story, I was quite clear that poetry would not do. The bookseller strongly recommended one, but when I found that it was written by the man whose works had already made two holidays miserable by their compulsory companionship I shook my head. However, he almost forced it upon me and refused, I am happy now to remember, to take my penny. I took it home and that night, by the light of a guttering candle, began to read. At first there were difficulties, the print was atrocious, very small and irregular, dark at one moment, faint at the other, and there were parallel columns to every page. But I struggled on; there was a curious sense of adventure connected with the affair; I had bought, or had at least tried to buy, this book with my very own money, the silence of the house all around me, the leaping flame of the candle, the cheesy smell of the brown cover, even the very smallness of the print excited me; this was a new experience.

Hugh Walpole, *These Diversions: Reading* (1926).

My own first visit to a real bookshop, as opposed to the paperback rack at the local drugstore, was to Barber's Bookstore in Fort Worth in March of 1954. I know it was in March because I took time off from a track meet, caught a bus downtown, and visited the bookshop, which is still there, still where it was then, a new bookshop that sold both new and used books. Six years later, while teaching at TCU, I found a very respectable copy of *The Catcher in the Rye* in a pile of junk on their floor. It cost me one dollar and is now worth about three thousand. In 1954 I had never heard of Salinger – indeed, had never heard of 98 percent of the authors whose books were in the second-hand part of Barber's Bookstore.

I had only two dollars to spend, on this my first trip to a real bookshop, and only about thirty minutes in which to make my choice, before heading back to the stadium, where, eventually, I ran a rather slow mile. Not knowing a thing about any of the books on the shelves, I was wholly at a loss, but as time was running out, I grabbed a copy of *Rogue Herries*, by Hugh Walpole. I had never heard of the author but I was looking for something modern and the book looked thoroughly modern to me . . . In November of 1998 I had a real book scout's epiphany – I bought the stock of Barber's Bookstore, and had the pleasure of packing the very shelf where that copy of *Rogue Herries* once had sat.

Larry McMurtry, *Walter Benjamin at the Dairy Queen* (1999).

At the little shop near Portland Road Station I came upon a first edition of Gibbon, the price an absurdity – I think it was a shilling volume. To possess those clean-paged quartos I would have sold my coat. As it happened, I had not money enough with me, but sufficient at home. I was living at Islington. Having spoken with the bookseller, I walked home, took the cash, walked back again, and – carried the tomes from the west end of Euston Road to a street in Islington far beyond the Angel. I did it in two journeys – this being the only time in my life when I thought of Gibbon in avoirdupois. Twice – three times, reckoning the walk for the money – did I descend Euston Road and climb Pentonville on that occasion. Of the season and the weather I have no recollection; my joy in the purchase I had made drove out every other thought. Except, indeed, of the weight. I had infinite energy, but not much muscular strength, and the end of the last journey saw me upon a chair, perspiring, flaccid, aching – exultant!

George Gissing, *The Private Papers of Henry Ryecroft* (1903).

We still find ourselves halting as instinctively at the humblest, or even the most familiar book-stall, as we used to do when fresh from school. In vain have we got cold feet at it, shivering, wind-beaten sides, and black-fingered gloves. The dusty old siren still delays us, charming with immortal beauty inside her homely attire, and singing songs of old poets. We still find ourselves diving even into the sixpenny or threepenny 'box', in spite of eternal disappointment, and running over whole windows of books, which we saw but three days before for the twentieth time, and of which we could repeat by heart a good third of the titles. Nothing disconcerts but absolute dirt, or an ill-tempered looking woman.

Leigh Hunt, 'Old books and bookshops: the beneficence of book-stalls' (1837).

Then yesterday, McIlwain and I went down to Oxford and had a great time book-hunting all day. I can't say we made any epoch-making discoveries, though we seem to have spent eight or ten pounds between us; but we had that peculiar thrill which comes from going into a room redolent with the faint mustiness of old calf and feeling that almost any volume may turn out a treasure.

Howard J. Laski, letter to Justice Holmes, 13 June, 1926.

I am an incurable book-collector and have haunted the antiquarian bookshops for forty-five years; I still have on my shelves the first old book I ever bought: the tenth edition of a volume of sermons printed in 1744, which cost two pence and which, without wishing to boast, I claim is worth at least double today.

A. N. L. Munby, 'Book collecting in the 1930s' (1973).

It's against my principles to buy a book I haven't read, it's like buying a dress you haven't tried on.

Helene Hanff, letter to Frank Doel, 9 February, 1952.

In book-buying you not infrequently condone an extravagance by the reflection that this particular purchase will be a good investment, sordidly considered: that you are not squandering income but sinking capital. But you know all the time that you are lying.

Kenneth Grahame, 'Non libri sed liberi' (1894).

There are some knightly souls who even go so far as to make their visits to bookshops a kind of chivalrous errantry at large. They go in not because they need any certain volume, but because they feel that there may be some book that needs them.

Christopher Morley, 'On visiting bookshops' (1925).

When Providence throws a good book in my way, I bow to its decree and purchase it as an act of piety, if it is reasonably or unreasonably cheap.

Oliver Wendell Holmes, *The Poet at the Breakfast Table* (1872).

In the shop window you have promptly identified the cover with the title you were looking for. Following this visual trail, you have forced your way through the shop past the thick barricade of Books You Haven't Read, which were frowning at you from the tables and shelves, trying to cow you. But you know you must never allow yourself to be awed, that among them there extend for acres and acres the Books You Needn't Read, the Books Made For Purposes Other Than Reading, Books Read Even Before You Open Them Since They Belong To The Category Of Books Read Before Being Written. And thus you pass the outer girdle of ramparts, but then you are attacked by the infantry of the Books That If You Had More Than One Life You Would Certainly Also Read But Unfortunately Your Days Are Numbered. With a rapid manoeuvre you bypass them and move into the phalanxes of the Books You Mean To Read But There Are Others You Must Read First, the Books Too Expensive Now And You'll Wait Till They're Remaindered, the Books ditto When They Come Out In Paperback, Books You Can Borrow From Somebody, Books That Everybody's Read So It's As If You Had Read Them Too. Eluding these assaults, you come up beneath the towers of the fortress, where other troops are holding out:

the Books You've Been Planning To Read For Ages,

the Books You've Been Hunting For Years Without Success,

the Books Dealing With Something You're Working On At The Moment,

the Books You Want To Own So They'll Be Handy Just In Case,

the Books You Could Put Aside Maybe To Read This
Summer,

the Books You Need To Go With Other Books On Your
Shelves,

the Books That Fill You With Sudden, Inexplicable Curiosity, Not Easily Justified.

Now you have been able to reduce the countless embattled
troops to an array that is, to be sure, very large but still calculable
to a finite number; but this relative relief is then undermined by
the ambush of the Books Read Long Ago Which It's Now Time
To Reread and the Books You've Always Pretended To Have
Read And Now It's Time To Sit Down And Really Read Them.

Italo Calvino, *If on a Winter's Night a Traveller* (1979).

Don't you find you always get distracted when you enter a
bookshop? You go in on your lunch break, determined to seek
out a copy of *Willard and his Bowling Trophies* by Richard
Brautigan. Shouldn't take long: they've either got it or they
haven't, and there'll still be time to get to Marks and Spencer
for a sandwich. An hour later you're jogging back to the office,
hungry, dehydrated, and exhibiting brautiganlessness, having
been ambushed by a new edition of the Molesworth tetralogy.
And here's the shame of it – you've already read all the St
Custard's books at least three times before.

'I like to read', *The Guardian*, 29 May, 2004.

When I worked in a second-hand bookshop – so easily pictured, if you don't work in one, as a kind of paradise where
charming old gentlemen browse eternally among calf-bound
folios – the thing that chiefly struck me was the rarity of really
bookish people. Our shop had an exceptionally interesting
stock, yet I doubt whether ten per cent of our customers knew
a good book from a bad one. First edition snobs were much
commoner than lovers of literature, but oriental students hag-

gling over cheap textbooks were commoner still, and vague-minded women looking for birthday presents for their nephews were commonest of all.

George Orwell, 'Bookshop memories' (1936).

Today one of those women who never know titles came into the shop. They are the source of Knightsbridge lady soup and they ask for a good book for a nephew or something new on roses for a gardening husband. This one wanted a novel, 'something for a good read at the cottage'. I offered her *Procurer to the King* by Fallopia Bothways. Going like a bomb with the menopausal set. She gasped, and I realized that I'd actually spoken the thought aloud: 'Going like a bomb with the menopausal set.'

She went quite red. 'What did you say?' she said.

'Going like a bomb, it's the best she's written yet,' I said, and looked very dim.

Russell Hoban, *Turtle Diary* (1975).

* * * * *

Charing Cross Road was for spotty adolescence. It flowed south from Tottenham Court Road like some fertilizing fog-yellow swamp bearing its cargo of highbrow culture and lowbrow sex. Here were the wonderful bookshops displaying in their windows recent publications and clasping in their innards second-hand classics: the collected works of Ruskin, Carlyle, Meredith, Macaulay et cetera et cetera, bought by the yard by the book-seller from the descendants of families that once had great premises boasting great libraries.

Here was Foyle's for everything, Collets with left-wing books as sharp as sickles, Zwemmer's for wonders of modern art (and a very amusing, highly updated, opinionated shop assistant called Rudolph Friedman), and perhaps a glimpse of grandiose Mr Zwemmer himself in canary-coloured waistcoat, looking fresh from some deal in Paris with Picasso.

At the south end of Charing Cross Road were the bargains-to-be, not yet quite ripened into full rarity: Grant Richardson's edition of Samuel Butler's *Erewhon* and *The Way of all Flesh*, first editions of Henry James (the worst-selling novelist with a great reputation of his time). One bookshop had a tub in the street, a kind of lucky dip of books all priced at sixpence. Once I drew out of this a French paperback novel by Jean Cocteau inscribed in the poet's very distinctive handwriting: 'A l'editeur du Times Literary Supplement avec les compliments de Jean Cocteau.'

Stephen Spender, *The Independent Magazine*, 18 November, 1989.

The Imperial Book Depot was one of the two best bookshops in town, and was located on Nabiganj, the fashionable street that was the last bulwark of modernity before the labyrinthine alleys and ancient, cluttered neighbourhoods of Old Brahmpur. Though it was a couple of miles away from the university proper it had a greater following among students and teachers than the University and Allied Bookshop, which was just a few minutes away from campus. The Imperial Book Depot was run by two brothers, Yashwant and Balwant, both almost illiterate in English, but both (despite their prosperous roundness) so energetic and entrepreneurial that it apparently made no difference. They had the best stock in town, and were extremely helpful to their customers. If a book was not available in the shop, they asked the customer himself to write down its name on the appropriate order form.

Twice a week an impoverished university student was paid to sort new arrivals onto the designated shelves. And since the bookshop prided itself on its academic as well as general stock, the proprietors unashamedly collared university teachers who wandered in to browse, sat them down with a cup of tea and a couple of publishers' lists, and made them tick off titles that they thought the bookshop should consider ordering. These teachers were happy to ensure that books they needed for their courses would be readily available to their students. Many of them resented the University and Allied Bookshop for its entrenched, lethargic, unresponsive and high-handed ways.

Vikram Seth, *A Suitable Boy* (1993).

It was an unusually respectable bookshop for this area of Soho, quite unlike the bookshop which faced it across the street and bore the simple sign 'Books' in scarlet letters. The window below the scarlet sign displayed girlie magazines which nobody was ever seen to buy – they were like a signal in an easy code long broken; they indicated the nature of private wares and interests inside. But the shop of Halliday & Son confronted the scarlet 'Books' with a window full of Penguins and Everyman and second-hand copies of World's Classics. The son was never seen there, only old Mr Halliday himself, bent and white-haired, wearing an air of courtesy like an old suit in which he would probably like to be buried.

Graham Greene, *The Human Factor* (1978).

The average man's notion of the book market is a beautiful shop-window, with rows of beautiful new books in speckless and variegated cloth bindings, and complete sets of established authors in morocco, calf, and Russia, and large illustrated volumes opened temptingly at a picture, and editions de luxe dotted about, and vistas of the Temple Classics in leather just to give a contrast to the portliness of the rest. And inside the shop, which is as religiously dim as a church, are all the latest things, and polished assistants incessantly engaged in taking twenty-five per cent off six shillings.

Arnold Bennett, 'Alone in London' (1902).

The ability to remember exactly where books are is a skill vital to the serious book scout – but it is such a peculiar skill that one suspects it must be genetically determined. Our own shop in Georgetown has been thought to be a very chaos by impatient customers who come in expecting the books to be neatly alphabetized, which, mostly, they aren't. I have long been a disciple of the Dusty Miller school of book shelving. Dusty Miller was a much admired London bookseller, who when asked how he arranged his books, replied that if he bought a short fat book he tried to find a short fat hole.

Larry McMurtry, *Walter Benjamin at the Dairy Queen* (1999).

Florence Green stocks her bookshop:

Although she had been trained never to look inside the books while at work, she opened one or two of them – old Everyman editions in faded olive boards stamped with gold. There was the elaborate endpaper which she had puzzled over when she was a little girl. A good book is the precious life-blood of a master spirit, embalmed and treasured up on purpose to a life beyond life. After some hesitation, she put it between Religion and Home Medicine.

Penelope Fitzgerald, *The Bookshop* (1978).

Twice a week Linda worked in a Red bookshop. It was run by a huge, perfectly silent comrade, called Boris. Boris liked to get drunk from Thursday afternoon, which was closing day in that district, to Monday morning, so Linda said she would take it over on Friday and Saturday. An extraordinary transformation would then occur. The books and tracts which mouldered there month after month, getting damper and dustier until at last they had to be thrown away, were hurried into the background, and their place taken by Linda's own few but well-loved favourites. Thus for *Whither British Airways?* was substituted *Around the World in 40 Days*, *Karl Marx, the Formative Years* was replaced by *The Making of a Marchioness*, and *The Giant of the Kremlin* by *Diary of a Nobody* while *A Challenge to Coal-Owners* made way for *King Solomon's Mines*.

Nancy Mitford, *The Pursuit of Love* (1945).

It is the loveliest old shop straight out of Dickens, you would go absolutely out of your mind over it.

There are stalls outside and I stopped and leafed through a few things just to establish myself as a browser before wandering in. It's dim inside, you smell the shop before you see it, it's a lovely smell, I can't articulate it easily, but it combines must and dust and age, and walls of wood and floors of wood. Toward the back of the shop at the left there's a desk with a work-lamp on it, a man was sitting there, he was about fifty with a Hogarth nose, he looked up and said 'Good afternoon?' in a North Country accent and I said I just wanted to browse and he said please do.

The shelves go on forever. They go up to the ceiling and they're very old and kind of grey, like old oak that has absorbed so much dust over the years they no longer are their true colour.

Maxine, letter to Helene Hanff, 10 September, 1951.

The truth is that even big collections of ordinary books distort space, as can readily be proved by anyone who has been around a really old-fashioned secondhand bookshop, one of those that look as though they were designed by M. Escher on a bad day and has more staircases than storeys and those rows of shelves which end in little doors that are surely too small for a full-sized human to enter.

Terry Pratchett, *Guards! Guards!* (1989).

Henry stood in the bright, clean shop, gazing at the disturbed corner from which books had been taken.

'My dear, you're ruining my business,' he said mildly and blandly.

'Henry!' She stopped near the foot of the stairs, as it were thunderstruck by a revelation.

'You don't understand how much of it depends on me having lots of books lying about as if they weren't anything at all.

That's just what book-collectors like. If everything was ship-shape they wouldn't look twice at the place. Whenever they see a pile of books in the dark they think there must be bargains.'

Arnold Bennett, *Riceyman Steps* (1923).

As a rule a bookshop is horribly cold in winter, because if it is too warm the windows get misted over, and a bookseller lives on his windows. And books give off more and nastier dust than any other class of objects yet invented, and the top of a book is the place where every bluebottle prefers to die.

George Orwell, 'Bookshop memories' (1936).

* * * * *

No man – no human, masculine, natural man – ever sells a book. Men have been known in moments of thoughtlessness, or compelled by temporary necessity, to rob, to equivocate, to do murder, to adventure themselves in the neighbourhood of fire-escapes: these things, howbeit regrettable, are common to human-ity, and may happen to any of us. But amateur bookselling is foul and unnatural; and it is noteworthy that our language, so capable of particularity, contains no distinctive name for the crime. Fortu-nately it is hardly known to exist: the face of the public being set against it as a flint – and the trade giving such wretched prices.

Kenneth Grahame, 'Non libri sed liberi' (1894).

Chandler drove hard bargains, and his understanding of books was so different from mine that I barely knew what to say to him. For me, books were not the containers of words so much as the words themselves, and the value of a given book was determined by its spiritual quality rather than its physical condition. A dog-eared Homer was worth more than a spanking Virgil, for example; three volumes of Descartes were worth less than one by Pascal. Those were essential distinctions for me, but for Chandler they did not exist. A book was no more than an object to him, a thing that belonged to the world of things, and as such it was not radically different from a shoebox, a toilet plunger, or a coffeepot. Each time I brought in another portion of Uncle Victor's library, the old man would go into his routine. Fingering the books with contempt, perusing the spines, hunting for marks and blemishes, he never failed to give the impression of someone handling a pile of filth. That was how the game worked. By degrading the goods, Chandler could offer rock-bottom prices. After thirty years of practice, he had the pose down pat, a repertoire of mutterings and asides, of wincings, tongue-clicks, and sad shakes of the head. The act was designed to make me feel the worthlessness of my own judgement, to shame me into recognizing the audacity of having presented these books to him in the first place. Are you telling me you want money for these things? Do you expect money from the garbage man when he carts away your trash?

Paul Auster, *Moon Palace* (1990).

* * * * *

The giving a Bookseller his Price for his Books has this Advantage: he that will do so, shall have the refusal of whatsoever comes to his hand, and so by that means get many things, which otherwise he never should have seen. So 'tis in giving a Baud her price.

John Selden, *The Table-Talk of John Selden* (1689).

One of the shop-windows he paused before was that of a second-hand book-shop, where, on a narrow table outside, the literature of the ages was represented in judicious mixture, from the immortal verse of Homer to the mortal prose of the railway novel. That the mixture was judicious was apparent from Deronda's finding in it something that he wanted – namely, that wonderful bit of autobiography, the life of the Polish Jew, Salomon Maimon; which, as he could easily slip into his pocket, he took from its place, and entered the shop to pay for, expecting to see behind the counter a grimy personage showing that nonchalance about sales which seems to belong universally to the second-hand book-business. In most other trades you find generous men who are anxious to sell you their wares for your own welfare; but even a Jew will not urge Simson's Euclid on you with an affectionate assurance that you will have pleasure in reading it, and that he wishes he had twenty more of the article, so much is it in request. One is led to fear that a second-hand bookseller may belong to that unhappy class of men who have no belief in the good of what they get their living by, yet keep conscience enough to be morose rather than unctuous in their vocation.

George Eliot, *Daniel Deronda* (1876).

I learnt early about the sturdy individualism of book-sellers. There was old Mr Matthews in the Arcade in Bristol who had filled his shop so full of books he had to sit outside on the pavement, wearing a tweed Norfolk hat. I did not ever see him sell a book.

A. N. L. Munby, 'Book collecting in the 1930s' (1973).

. . . EXCLUDED BY THE POP DEMAND as is the shop nearly opp. One day I was in there and I could see a bk I knew at the top of a pile, out of reach. I asked if there was a ladder, the owner said no. I stood on my bag & then jumped & got the bk, it was exactly the one I wanted, I asked how much? It's not for sale, he said as he came over and took it out of my hand and thus revealed that he had been standing in front of the ladder.

B. C. M. Driffield, *Driff's Guide to All the Secondhand Bookshops in Britain* (1985).

One reason the owners of those aforesaid little rambling, poky second-hand bookshops always seem slightly unearthly is that many of them are, having strayed into this world after taking a wrong turning in their own bookshops in worlds where it is considered commendable business practice to wear carpet slippers all the time and open your shop only when you feel like it.

Terry Pratchett, Guards! Guards! (1989).

I can't really even try to put on paper the glories of this old fellow. Imagine a vast physique, a stinking clay pipe with a long stem, a beard which waved with excitement when he spoke, and trousers so baggy and wide that I sometimes wondered if he kept books in them.

Howard J. Laski, letter to Justice Holmes, 26 August, 1925.

I had also one good book hunt which was grand. Imagine a shop cellar in a slum near Houndsditch. The books were without order in vertical columns on the floor. The man might have been the offspring of a marriage between Fagin and Mrs Gamp; for he was in a kind of perpetual moisture from gin, and he constantly shot round corners of the shop as though on guard to see that one stole no books.

Howard J. Laski, letter to Justice Holmes, 26 December, 1933.

I have two favourite parts of the day. The first is where I open up in expectation of welcoming new friends and old friends to my little palace of books. People come back after 30, 40, 50 years, with happy memories, to see what's changed. The second moment is at midnight, when I close and I can take six books – they're like jewels, I feel like a gold-miner who's struck it rich – to my room to read before I go to sleep.

George Whitman, 'A life in the day' (2004).

When we went to the country, I would play at being a bookseller; I entitled the silvery leaf of the birch *The Azure Queen*, and the varnished leaf of the magnolia *Flower of the Snows*; I arranged some scholarly displays of my stock. I wasn't sure whether when I was grown-up I wanted to write books or sell them, but in my view they were the most precious things in the world.

Simone de Beauvoir, *Memoirs of a Dutiful Daughter* (1958).

* * * * *

. . . the fine flare of one of Mr W. H. Smith's bookstalls – a feature not to be omitted in any enumeration of the charms of Paddington and Euston. It is a focus of warmth and light in the vast smoky cavern; it gives the idea that literature is a thing of splendour, of a dazzling essence, of infinite gas-lit red and gold. A glamour hangs over the glittering booth, and a tantalising air of clever new things. How brilliant must the books all be, how veracious and courteous the fresh, pure journals! Of a Saturday afternoon, as you wait in your corner of the compartment for the starting of the train, the window makes a frame for the glowing picture.

Henry James, 'London' (1888).

A sunk railway track and a gin distillery flank the gritty street. There is something Victorian about the whole place – an air of ugly commercial endeavour mixed with odd idealisms and philanthropies. It isn't only the jumble of unattractive titles on the dusty spines, the huge weight of morality at sixpence a time; even the setting has an earnestness . . . The public-houses are like a lesson in temperance.

It isn't all books by any means in the book market: a dumb man presides over the first stall given over to paintbrushes and dividers; we pass wireless parts, rubber heels, old stony collections of nuts and bolts, gramophone records, cycle tyres, spectacles (hospital prescriptions made up on the spot under the shadow of the gin distillery), a case of broken (I was going to say moth-eaten) butterflies – privet-hawks and orange-tips and red admirals losing their antennae and powder, shabby like second-hand clothes. One stall doesn't display its wares at all: only labels advertising Smell Bombs, Itching Powder, Cigarette Bangs – Victorian too, the painful physical humour, reminding us of Cruikshank on the poor and Gilbert on old age.

And then at last the books. It is a mistake to look for bargains here, or even to hope to find any books you really want – unless you happen to want Thackeray, Froude, or Macaulay on the cheap. These authors are ubiquitous. No, the book market is the place for picking up odd useless information. Here, for instance, is *Dibden's Purification of Sewage and Water*, published by the Sanitary Publishing Company, next to *Spiritual Counsel for District Visitors*, *Submarine Cables*, and *Chicago Police Problems*, published – it seems broadminded – by the Chicago University Press. Of course, there are folios called *View of the Lakes* or *of Italy, Switzerland, the Tyrol*, as the case may be; and one can buy, in pale-blue paper parts, *Bessemer on Working Blast Furnaces*. *Doll Caudel in Paris* seems to be part of a series and looks a little coarse.

Graham Greene, 'Book market' (1951).

'Sahib. Latest from Plato. *The Republic*. Also, James Hadley Chase and P. G. Wodehouse. You want *Catcher in the Rye*, sahib? *MAD* magazine? But sahib, just now unpacked. At least sample *Little Dorrit* by Charles Dickens.'

To me, that is what is meant to learn to read in India. Having the pleasures of reading shouted at you from pavement booksellers before you even knew how to read. Envying the animation on the face of the grown-up bent over the volumes displayed on a threadbare carpet by the roadside while the bookseller slapped another two books together to loosen the dust kicked up by passing pedestrians, before whispering, '*Anna Karenina*, sahib, *Madame Bovary*. Hot books only this very minute arrived. Believe it or not, sahib. Tomorrow no copies remaining!'

Gita Mehta (1992).

* * * * *

... the following advertisement appeared in the Salterton evening paper ...

We are directed by Miss Valentine Rich, executor of the late Dr Savage, to announce that his splendid library, comprising more than 4300 volumes of Philosophy, Theology, Travel, Superior Fiction and Miscellaneous will be open to the clergy of all denominations from 10 o'clock Wednesday, June 6th, and they may have gratis any volumes they choose. This is done in accordance with the wish of the late Dr Savage. Clergy must remove books personally.

ELLIOT AND MAYBEE
Auctioneers and Valuers

Anything which concerns a subject dear to us seems to leap from a large page of print. Freddy Webster, who was no careful reader of newspapers, saw it, and snorted like a young warhorse.

'Giving away books!' said she. 'But only to preachers! Damn!'

Later that evening she met Solly ...

'Yes, I saw it,' he said in answer to her question. 'Pretty rotten, confining it to the clergy. Not that I care about Philosophy, or Theology, or even Superior Fiction. But there might just be something tucked away in Miscellaneous which would be lost on the gentlemen of the cloth.'

'Whatever made Valentine do it?'

'Apparently, two or three years ago, the old chap said something, just in passing, about wanting his books dealt with that way. And they're quite unsaleable, you know. A bookseller wouldn't give five cents apiece for the lot.'

'Have you seen them, Solly?'

'No; but you know how hard it is to get rid of books. Especially Theology. Nothing changes fashion so quickly as Theology.'

'But there might just be a treasure or two among them.'

'I know.'

'Still, I don't suppose a preacher would know a really valuable book if he saw one. They'll go for the concordances and commentaries on the Gospels. Do you suppose Val would let us look through what's left?'

'Freddy, my innocent poppet, there won't be anything left. They'll strip the shelves. Anything free has an irresistible fascination. Free books to preachers will be like free booze to politicians; they'll scoop the lot, without regard for quality. You mark my words.'

Freddy recognized the truth of what he said. She herself was a victim of that lust for books which rages in the breast like a demon, and which cannot be stilled save by the frequent and plentiful acquisition of books. This passion is more common, and more powerful, than most people suppose. Book lovers are thought by unbookish people to be gentle and unworldly, and perhaps a few of them are so. But there are others who will lie and scheme and steal to get books as wildly and unconscionably as the dope-taker in pursuit of his drug. They may not want the books to read immediately, or at all; they want them to possess, or to range on their shelves, to have at command. They want books as a Turk is thought to want concubines – not to be hastily deflowered, but to be kept at their master's call, and enjoyed more often in thought than in reality. Solly was in a measure a victim of this unscrupulous passion, but Freddy was wholly in the grip of it.

Still, she had her pride. She would not beg Valentine to regard her as a member of the clergy for a day; she would not even hang about the house in a hinting manner. She would just drop in, and if the conversation happened to turn upon books, as some scholarly rural dean fingered a rare volume, she would let it be known, subtly, that she was deeply interested in them, and then – well, and then she would see what happened.

With this plan in view she was at the residence of the late Dr Adam Savage at five minutes to ten on the following morning, dismayed to find that an astounding total of two hundred and seventeen clergymen were there before her, waiting impatiently on the lawn. They ranged from canons of the cathedral, in shovel hats and the gray flannels which the more worldly Anglicans affect in summer, through Presbyterians and ministers of the United Church in black coats and Roman collars, to the popes and miracle workers of backstreet sects, dressed in everything under the sun. There was a young priest, a little aloof from the others, who had been instructed by his bishop to bespeak a copy of *The Catholic Encyclopaedia* which was known to be in the house, for a school library. There were two rabbis, one with a beard and one without, chatting with the uneasy geniality of men who expect shortly to compete in a race for a shelf of books on the Pentateuch . . . There was no representative of the Greek Orthodox, the Syrian or Coptic Churches; otherwise Christianity in its utmost variety was assembled on that lawn . . .

At five minutes past ten, when the clergy were beginning to buzz like bees, a car stopped in front of the lawn and young Mr Maybee and Valentine climbed out of it. They were a good deal surprised and discomposed to find a crowd waiting for them, and hurried to open the front door. It had been their intention to sit quietly in the library at a table, arranging some final details of the sale and welcoming the occasional clergyman who might drop in for a book. Instead they were closely followed up the steps, not rudely, but as cattle follow a farmer with a pail of hot mash. When the door was opened the clergy increased their pace, still without rudeness, but with a kind of hungry fervour, and Valentine and young Mr Maybee found that they were entering the library at a brisk trot. It was a room of moderate size, and might perhaps have held fifty people when full. Seventy rushed into it in sixty seconds, and the remainder crowded as close to the entry as they could.

One does not describe the activity of clergymen in a library as looting. They were, in the main, quiet and well-bred men, and it was in a quiet and well-bred manner that they went to work. The pushing was of a moderate order, and the phrase 'Excuse me' was often heard. Natural advantages, such as long arms, superior height, and good eyesight were given rein, but there was no actual snatching nor were the old intentionally trodden upon. No very wide choice, no thoughtful ranging of the shelves, was possible in such a crush, and with good-humoured philosophy the visitors seized whatever was nearest. There were a few friendly disagreements; a shovel hat and the brown suit had each got hold of five volumes of a nicely bound ten-volume set of the works of a Scottish metaphysician, and neither could see why the other should not yield his portion. The rabbis, pushed in a corner where there was little but New Testament material, struggled feebly to reach their Promised Land, without knowing precisely where it was to be found. The young priest found his encyclopaedia, but it was too bulky to be moved at one time, and he knew that it would be fatal to leave any part of it behind him, in the hope of making a second trip. An elderly Presbyterian fainted, and young Mr Maybee had to appeal in a loud voice for help to lift him through the window into the open air; Valentine took her chance to crawl out onto the lawn, in the wake of the invalid.

'What shall we do?' she asked the auctioneer, who was a nice young man, and supposedly accustomed to dominating crowds.

'God knows,' said Mr Maybee; 'I've never seen anything like it.' . . .

By half-past eleven two hundred and thirty-six clergymen had passed through the library, some of them three or four times, and the shelves were bare. Dr Savage's bequest had been somewhat liberally interpreted, for an inkwell, a pen tray, two letter files, two paperweights, a small bust of Homer, a packet of blotters and an air-cushion which had been in the swivel chair were gone, as well. The widest interpretation had been placed on the word 'library' in the advertisement, for some of the visitors had invaded the upstairs regions and made off with two or three hundred detective novels which had been in the old scholar's bedroom. Even a heap of magazines in the cellarway had been removed.

'I don't think there's a scrap of printed matter left in the house,' said young Mr Maybee.

Robertson Davies, Tempest-Tost (1951).

* * * * *

It would be a good thing to buy books if one could also buy the time to read them; but one usually confuses the purchase of books with the acquisition of their contents.

Arthur Schopenhauer, 'On books and writing' (1851).

8. 'IN CONSTANT CIRCULATION': BORROWING, LENDING AND SHARING

The people who shelve the books in Widener talk about the library's *breathing* – at the start of term, the stacks exhale books in great swirling clouds; at the end of term, the library inhales, and the books fly back. So the library is a body, too, the pages of books pressed together like organs in the darkness.

Matthew Battles, *Library: An Unquiet History* (2003).

'You see, Brother William,' the abbot said, 'to achieve the immense and holy task that enriches those walls' – and he nodded toward the bulk of the Aedificium, which could be glimpsed from the cell's windows, towering above the abbatial church itself – 'devout men have toiled for centuries, observing iron rules. The library was laid out on a plan which has remained obscure to all over the centuries, and which none of the monks is called upon to know. Only the librarian has received the secret, from the librarian who preceded him, and he communicates it, while still alive, to the assistant librarian, so that death will not take him by surprise and rob the community of that knowledge. And the secret seals the lips of both men. Only the librarian has, in addition to that knowledge, the right to move through the labyrinth of the books, he alone knows where to find them and where to replace them, he alone is responsible for their safekeeping. The other monks work in the scriptorium and may know the list of the volumes that the library houses. But a list of titles often tells very little; only the librarian knows, from the collocation of the volume, from its degree of inaccessibility, what

secrets, what truths or falsehoods, the volume contains. Only
he decides how, when, and whether to give it to the monk
who requests it; sometimes he first consults me. Because not
all truths are for all ears, not all falsehoods can be recognised
as such by a pious soul; and the monks, finally, are in the
scriptorium to carry out a precise task, which requires them
to read certain volumes and not others, and not to pursue
every foolish curiosity that seizes them, whether through
weakness of intellect or through pride or through diabolical
prompting.'

Umberto Eco, The Name of the Rose (1983).

I was one summer's day loitering through the great saloons
of the British Museum, with that listlessness with which one
is apt to saunter about a museum in warm weather; sometimes lolling over a glass case of minerals, sometimes studying
the hieroglyphics on an Egyptian mummy, and sometimes
trying, with nearly equal success, to comprehend the allegori-
cal paintings on the lofty ceilings. Whilst I was gazing about
in this idle way, my attention was attracted to a distant door,
at the end of a suite of apartments. It was closed, but every
now and then it would open, and some strange-favoured
being, generally clothed in black, would steal forth, and glide
through the rooms, without noticing any of the surrounding
objects. There was an air of mystery about this that piqued
my languid curiosity, and I determined to attempt the passage
of that strait, and to explore the unknown regions beyond.
The door yielded to my hand, with that facility with which
the portals of enchanted castles yield to the adventurous
knight-errant. I found myself in a spacious chamber, surrounded with great cases of venerable books. Above the
cases, and just under the cornice, were arranged a great
number of black-looking portraits of ancient authors. About
the room were placed long tables, with stands for reading and

writing, at which sat many pale, studious personages, poring intently over dusty volumes, rummaging among mouldy manuscripts, and taking copious notes of their contents. A hushed stillness reigned through this mysterious apartment, excepting that you might hear the racing of pens over sheets of paper, or occasionally, the deep sigh of one of these sages, as he shifted his position to turn over the page of an old folio: doubtless arising from that hollowness and flatulency incident to learned research.

Now and then one of these personages would write something on a small slip of paper, and ring a bell, whereupon a familiar would appear, take the paper in profound silence, glide out of the room, and return shortly loaded with ponderous tomes, upon which the other would fall tooth and nail with famished voracity.

I was, in fact, in the reading-room of the great British Library – an immense collection of volumes of all ages and languages, many of which are now forgotten, and most of which are seldom read.

Washington Irving, 'The art of book-making' (1820–1).

*****

And the smell of the library was always the same – the musty odour of old clothes mixed with the keener scent of unwashed bodies, creating what the chief librarian had once described as 'the steam of the social soup'.

Peter Ackroyd, *Chatterton* (1987).

The librarian now stepped up to me, and demanded whether I had a card of admission. At first I did not comprehend him, but I soon found that the library was a kind of literary 'preserve,' subject to game-laws, and that no one must presume to hunt there without special licence and permission. In a word, I stood convicted of being an arrant poacher, and was glad to make a precipitate retreat, lest I should have a whole pack of authors let loose upon me.

Washington Irving, 'The art of book-making' (1820–1).

The Librarian is, of course, very much in favour of reading in general, but readers in particular get on his nerves. There is something sacrilegious about the way people keep taking books off the shelves and wearing out the words by reading them. He likes people who love and respect books, and the best way to do that, in the Librarian's opinion, is to leave them on the shelves where Nature intended them to be.

Terry Pratchett and Stephen Briggs, *The Discworld Companion* (1994).

One librarian thought my books were far too popular and the hoards of children swarming into the library for them on Saturday morning became a nuisance. 'If only you could see the children swamping the shelves,' he told me. 'It makes us far too busy.'

Enid Blyton, quoted in *Birmingham Evening Mail*, 3 November, 1964.

Miss Villets emphatically stamped a date in the front of *Frank on the Lower Mississippi* for a small flaxen boy, glowering at him as though she were stamping a warning on his brain.

Sinclair Lewis, *Main Street: The Story of Carol Kennicott* (1920).

LIBRARIAN

Overdue again! Seven reminders I've sent out to you!

HANCOCK

My dear good fellow. One cannot rush one's savouring of the classics of world literature. Rome was not built in a day and its decline and fall cannot be read in one.

LIBRARIAN

But you haven't got Gibbon's *Decline and Fall* there.

HANCOCK

That's got nothing to do with it. I've got *The Love Lives of the Caesars* here and that tells me everything.

Alan Simpson and Ray Galton, *Hancock's Half Hour: The Missing Page* (1960).

And my experience with public libraries is that the first volume of the book I inquire for is out, unless I happen to want the second, when *that* is out.

Oliver Wendell Holmes, *The Poet at the Breakfast Table* (1872)

The librarian was not an undecent sort, and bought me books by Dickens that I had asked for. It was not much good asking for modern authors because they did not have any. It was my belief they bought the books for the prison by weight. I once got a *Chums* annual for 1917 and a Selfridge's furniture catalogue for my non-fiction or educational book.

Brendan Behan, *Borstal Boy* (1958).

* * * * *

Libraries are reservoirs of strength, grace and wit, reminders of order, calm and continuity, lakes of mental energy, neither warm nor cold, light nor dark. The pleasure they give is steady, unorgastic, reliable, deep and long-lasting. In any library in the world, I am at home, unselfconscious, still and absorbed.

Germaine Greer, *Daddy, We Hardly Knew You* (1990).

* * * * *

The learned world may very fairly be divided into those who return books borrowed by them, and those who do not.

John Hill Burton, *The Book-Hunter* (1862).

When I get hold of a book I particularly admire, I am so enthusiastic that I loan it to someone who never brings it back.

Edgar Watson Howe, *Country Town Sayings* (1911).

There is no tribe of human beings more pestiferous than the people who insist on lending you books, whether you wish to borrow them or not. They thrust them upon you as you are leaving, with an enthusiasm that would make it seem a rudeness to refuse. I confess I have no taste for other people's books, and I do not like carrying them about in 'buses and tubes and taxis, and I like still less carrying them when I am walking. I do not, as a rule, even wish to read them. I have no time to read my own books . . . – why, then, should I wish to read other people's? Yet, if I borrow a book, I cannot abstain from reading it with a pricking of conscience every time I see it and I cannot help seeing it every time I am looking for something else.

Robert Lynd, 'Out of print' (1923).

Books are one of the few things men cherish deeply. And the better the man the more easily will he part with his most cherished possessions. A book lying idle on a shelf is wasted ammunition. Like money, books must be kept in constant circulation. Lend and borrow to the maximum – of both books and money! But especially books, for books represent infinitely more than money. A book is not only a friend, it makes friends for you. When you have possessed a book with mind and spirit, you are enriched. But when you pass it on you are enriched threefold.

Henry Miller, 'They were alive and they spoke to me' (1969).

Some people are unwilling to lend their books. I have a special grudge against them, particularly those who accompany their unwillingness with uneasy professions to the contrary.

Leigh Hunt, 'My books' (1823).

Hard-covered books break up friendships. You loan a hard-covered book to a friend and when he doesn't return it you get mad at him. It makes you mean and petty. But twenty-five cent books are different.

John Steinbeck (1954).

*****

I love reading good plays; and so does M. We have such fun talking them over afterwards. In fact, the pleasure of all reading is doubled when one lives with another who shares the same books. It is one of the many pleasures of our solitary life.

Katherine Mansfield, letter to Lady Ottoline Morrell, January 1922.

I learned very early that when you were infatuated with someone, you read the same books the other person read or you read the books that had shaped the other person or you committed an infidelity and read for yourself and it was the beginning of trouble.

Harold Brodkey, 'Reading: the most dangerous game' (1985).

Promising to love each other for richer or for poorer, in sickness and in health – even promising to forsake all others – had been no problem, but it was a good thing the *Book of Common Prayer* didn't say anything about marrying our libraries and throwing out the duplicates. That would have been a far more solemn vow, one that would probably have caused the wedding to grind to a mortifying halt.

Anne Fadiman, *Ex Libris: Confessions of a Common Reader* (1998).

INTERIOR. ALVY'S LIVING ROOM – DAY.
A lighted Christmas tree stands in the middle of boxes, books and the general disarray of packing and figuring out what belongs to whom as Alvy helps Annie move out.

ALVY (*Holding up a book*)
Whose *Catcher in the Rye* is this?
ANNIE (*Walking into the room with an armload of books*)
Well, let's see now . . . If it has my name on it, then I guess it's mine.
ALVY (*Reacting*)
Oh, it sure has . . . You know, you wrote your name in all my books, 'cause you knew this day was gonna come.
ANNIE (*Putting down the books and flipping back her hair*)
Well, uh, Alvy, you wanted to break up just as much as I do.
ALVY (*Riffling through the books*)
There's no-no question in my mind. I think we're doing the mature thing, without any doubt.
ANNIE (*Holding a framed picture and moving about*)
Now, look, all the books on death and dying are yours and all the poetry books are mine.
ALVY (*Looking down at a book*)
This *Denial of Death*. You remember this?
ANNIE
Oh –
ALVY
This is the first book that I got you.

Woody Allen, *Annie Hall* (1977).

9. 'A DISTINCTION OF SPECIES': WHAT TO READ, AND HOW

In other words what culture demands of us in our reading is simply a heightened sense of the grandeur of the epic of human life upon earth.

John Cowper Powys, *The Meaning of Culture* (1929)

For all books are divisible into two classes: the books of the hour, and the books of all time. Mark this distinction – it is not one of quality only. It is not merely the bad book that does not last, and the good one that does. It is a distinction of species. There are good books for the hour, and good ones for all time; bad books for the hour, and bad ones for all time.

John Ruskin, *Sesame and Lilies* (1864).

In order to read what is good one must make it a condition never to read what is bad; for life is short and both time and strength limited.

Arthur Schopenhauer, 'On reading and books' (1851).

Some books are undeservedly forgotten; none are undeservedly remembered.

W. H. Auden, 'Reading' (1963).

* * * * *

'Have you read *Brothers*?' Lady Kroesig asked Uncle Matthew, conversationally, as they settled down to their soup.

'What's that?'

'The new Ursula Langdok – 'Brothers' – it's about two brothers. You ought to read it.'

'My dear Lady Kroesig, I have only ever read one book in my life, and that is *White Fang*. It's so frightfully good I've never bothered to read another.'

Nancy Mitford, *The Pursuit of Love* (1945).

Always excepting the Oxford Dictionary. If you can manage to lift one of the volumes of this from its shelf, you will find it the best reading of all.

Rose Macaulay, *A Casual Commentary* (1925).

'I have a book for you to read.' She always has a book for me to read. She has a book about everything. She reads the first chapter and the table of contents and the last three paragraphs and if she likes the theory she says APPROVED and goes on to the next book.

If she really likes the theory she writes the author and the publisher and buys twenty copies and gives them away to friends. She has ruined a lot of books for me that way. What real book could live up to one of mother's glowing and inaccurate descriptions?

It must be interesting to be her daughter, people say to me.

I don't know, I tell them. I've never tried it. I use her for a librarian.

Ellen Gilchrist, 'Indignities' (1981).

And if she can have access to a good library of old and classical books, there need be no choosing at all. Keep the modern magazine and novel out of your girl's way; turn her loose into the old library every wet day, and let her alone. She will find what is good for her.

John Ruskin, *Sesame and Lilies* (1864).

From her earliest Youth she had discovered a Fondness for Reading, which extremely delighted the Marquis; he permitted her therefore the Use of his Library, in which, unfortunately, for her, were great Store of Romances, and, what was still more unfortunate, not in the original *French*, but very bad Translations.

Charlotte Lennox, *The Female Quixote* (1752).

Mrs Linnet had become an avid reader of religious books since Mr Tryan's advent, and as she was in the habit of confining her perusal to the purely secular portions, which bore a very small proportion to the whole, she could make rapid progress through a large number of volumes. On taking up the biography of a celebrated preacher, she immediately turned to the end to see what disease he died of; and if his legs swelled, as her own occasionally did, she felt a stronger interest in ascertaining any earlier facts in the history of the dropsical divine – whether he had ever fallen off a stage coach, whether he had married more than one wife, and, in general, any adventures or repartees recorded of him previous to the epoch of his conversion. She then glanced over the letters and diary, and wherever there was a predominance of Zion, the River of Life, and notes of exclamation, she turned over to the next page; but any passage in which she saw such promising nouns as 'smallpox,' 'pony,' or 'books and shoes,' at once arrested her.

George Eliot, 'Janet's Repentence' in *Scenes from Clerical Life* (1858).

About once a year some bright journal asks each of our leading men and women for a few lines on the topic, 'If I were forced to live on a desert island with permission to take only one book, what would that book be?' . . . [I]f they were truthful they would all select some manual in varnished picture-boards called *Practical Boat-Building for Amateurs*. If the aim is to discover what people like, the test is wrong, for the patients are all given a chance to show off when they return to civilisation. The real test is to promise anonymity for the replies, and ask: 'If you were the last survivor of the human race, what kind of book would you read?' Practically all of us would answer, 'Detective stories, till I had read every one three times; then humorous novels; then I should go to the bad, give up books, and read the private correspondence of my deceased neighbours and friends.'

Gilbert Norwood, 'Too many books' (1926).

* * * * *

Do your bit to save humanity from lapsing back into barbarity by reading all the novels you can.

Richard Hughes, speech at Foyle's literary luncheon, in honour of his
75th birthday, 1975.

'One trouble with books is that they're not so thoroughly safeguarded by intelligent censors as the movies are, and when you drop into the library and take out a book you never know what you're wasting your time on. What I like in books is a wholesome, really improving story, and sometimes – Why, once I started a novel by this fellow Balzac that you read about, and it told how a lady wasn't living with her husband, I mean she wasn't his wife. It went into details, disgustingly! And the English was real poor. I spoke to the library about it, and they took it off the shelves. I'm not narrow, but I must say I don't see any use in this deliberately dragging in immorality! Life itself is so full of temptations that in literature one wants only that which is pure and uplifting.'

Sinclair Lewis, *Main Street: The Story of Carol Kennicott* (1920).

Lady Peabury was in the morning-room reading a novel; early training gave a guilty spice to this recreation, for she had been brought up to believe that to read a novel before luncheon was one of the gravest sins it was possible for a gentlewoman to commit.

Evelyn Waugh, 'An Englishman's home' (1939).

. . . it is surely obvious that the butler's pantry must be the one place in the house where privacy and solitude are guaranteed.

As it happened, when she entered my pantry that evening, I was not in fact engaged in professional matters. That is to say, it was towards the end of the day during a quiet week and I had been enjoying a rare hour or so off duty. As I say, I am not certain if Miss Kenton entered with her vase of flowers, but I certainly do recall her saying:

'Mr Stevens, your room looks even less accommodating at night than it does in the day. That electric bulb is too dim, surely, for you to be reading by.'

'It is perfectly adequate, thank you, Miss Kenton.'

'Really, Mr Stevens, this room resembles a prison cell. All one needs is a small bed in the corner and one could well imagine condemned men spending their last hours here.'

Perhaps I said something to this, I do not know. In any case, I did not look up from my reading, and a few moments passed during which I waited for Miss Kenton to excuse herself and leave. But then I heard her say:

'Now I wonder what it could be that you are reading there, Mr Stevens.'

'Simply a book, Miss Kenton.'

'I can see that, Mr Stevens. But what sort of book – that is what interests me.'

I looked up to see Miss Kenton advancing towards me. I shut the book, and clutching it to my person, rose to my feet.

'Really, Miss Kenton,' I said, 'I must ask you to respect my privacy.'

'But why are you so shy about your book, Mr Stevens? I rather suspect it may be something rather racy.'

'It is quite out of the question, Miss Kenton, that anything "racy", as you put it, should be found on his Lordship's shelves.'

'I have heard it said that many learned books contain the most racy of passages, but I have never had the nerve to look. Now, Mr Stevens, do please allow me to see what it is you are reading.'

'Miss Kenton, I must ask you to leave me alone. It is quite impossible that you should persist in pursuing me like this during the very few moments of spare time I have to myself.'

But Miss Kenton was continuing to advance and I must say it was a little difficult to assess what my best course of action would be. I was tempted to thrust the book into the drawer of my desk and lock it, but this seemed absurdly dramatic. I took a few paces back, the book still held to my chest.

'Please show me the volume you are holding, Mr Stevens,' Miss Kenton said, continuing her advance, 'and I will leave you to the pleasures of your reading. What on earth can it be you are so anxious to hide?'

'Miss Kenton, whether or not you discover the title of this volume is in itself not of the slightest importance to me. But as a matter of principle, I object to your appearing like this and invading my private moments.'

'I wonder, is it a perfectly respectable volume, Mr Stevens, or are you in fact protecting me from its shocking influences?'

Then she was standing before me, and suddenly the atmosphere underwent a peculiar change – almost as though the two of us had been suddenly thrust on to some other plane of being altogether. I am afraid it is not easy to describe clearly what I mean here. All I can say is that everything around us suddenly became very still; it was my impression that Miss Kenton's manner also underwent a sudden change; there was a strange seriousness in her expression, and it struck me she seemed almost frightened.

'Please, Mr Stevens, let me see your book.'

She reached forward and began gently to release the volume from my grasp. I judged it best to look away while she did so, but with her person positioned so closely, this could only be achieved by my twisting my head away at a somewhat unnatural angle. Miss Kenton continued very gently to prise the book away, practically one finger at a time. The process seemed to take a very long time – throughout which I managed to maintain my posture – until finally I heard her say:

'Good gracious, Mr Stevens, it isn't anything so scandalous at all. Simply a sentimental love story.'

Kazuo Ishiguro, The Remains of the Day (1989).

*****

Does there, I wonder, exist a being who has read all, or approximately all, that the person of average culture is supposed to have read, and that not to have read is a social sin? If such a being does exist, surely he is an old, a very old man, who has read steadily that which he ought to have read sixteen hours a day, from early infancy. . . . My leisure has been moderate, my desire strong and steady, my taste in selection certainly above the average, and yet in ten years I seem scarcely to have made an impression upon the intolerable multitude of volumes which 'everyone is supposed to have read'.

Arnold Bennett, Journal, 15 October, 1896.

Inevitably there are some 'important' books I haven't read. This causes a dilemma when mixing with fellow readers at parties. But it is one easily resolved by harbouring a handful of well-rehearsed lines up your sleeve: 'The humour in *Private Life of an Indian Prince* by Mulk Raj Anand is somewhat perverse I've always thought'; 'Amos Tutuola's *The Palm-Wine Drunkard* for me epitomises Africa's unique contribution to the discipline'; 'All I ever needed to know about Britain's colonial exit strategy I discovered in Ngugi Wa Thiong'o's masterly *A Grain of Wheat*. Or perhaps you preferred *Petals of Blood*? Such a shame he took to writing in Kikuyu after that. I feel I miss some of the nuances.' Then edge towards the Twiglets.

'I like to read', *The Guardian*, 29 May, 2004

How useful it would be to have an authoritative list of books that, despite the world's generally high opinion of them, one really need not read: books generally overrated or overwritten – books that somehow or other do not come near repaying the time required to read them!

Joseph Epstein, 'The noblest distraction' (1985).

The Cream Theory finds its best expression in those dreadful lists of the World's Best Books. Everyone who has glanced through those catalogues knows how repellent they are; but does he realise why? It is because they are inhuman. The list is nobody's list, though it contains something which would be in everybody's list; it is the greatest common measure of Books That Have Helped. Just so one might compose a statue of the best head, the finest arm, etc., to be found among the world's sculptures. The catalogue will contain, let us say, the 'Sakuntala' and 'The Path to Rome'. Now both may be capital books, but the point is that nobody – no real individual person – reads both . . . It can't be done any more than you can be both a

jockey and a botanist. And any list, to be real, must, at whatever cost, correspond to some conceivable personality.

Gilbert Norwood, 'Too many books' (1926).

And this leads me to say how woefully mistaken are those
who believe that certain books, because universally acknowl-
edged as 'masterpieces', are the books which alone have
power to inspire and nourish us. Every lover of books can
name dozens of titles which, because they unlock his soul,
because they open his eyes to reality, are for him the golden
books. It matters not what evaluation is made of these by
scholars and critics, by pundits and authorities: for the man
who is touched to the quick by them they are supreme.

Henry Miller, 'Letter to Pierre Lesdain' (1969).

* * * * *

For casual reading – in your bath, for instance, or late at
night when you are too tired to go to bed, or in the odd
quarter of an hour before lunch – there is nothing to touch a
back number of the *Girl's Own Paper*.

George Orwell, 'Bookshop memories' (1936).

'Almost any book does for a bed-book,' a woman once said
to me. I nearly replied in a hurry that almost any woman
would do for a wife; but that is not the way to bring people to
conviction of sin.

H. M. Tomlinson, 'Bed-books and night-lights' (1918).

Anyway, poetry is not the most important thing in life, is it?
Frankly, I'd much rather lie in a hot bath sucking boiled
sweets and reading Agatha Christie.

Dylan Thomas, quoted by Joan Wyndham, *Love is Blue: A Wartime
Diary*, 6 July, 1943.

* * * * *

I like those great *still* books and I wish there were a great novel in hundreds of volumes that I might go on and on . . .

Alfred, Lord Tennyson, quoted by his son in *A Memoir* (1897).

* * * * *

There are books that one has for twenty years without reading them, that one always keeps at hand, that one takes from city to city, from country to country, carefully packed, even when there is very little room, and perhaps one leafs through them when removing them from a trunk; yet one carefully refrains from reading even a complete sentence. Then, after twenty years, there comes a moment when suddenly, as though under a very high compulsion, one cannot help taking in such a book from beginning to end, at one sitting: It is like a revelation. Now one knows why one made such a fuss about it. It had to be with one for a time; it had to travel; it has to occupy space; it had to be a burden; and now it has reached the goal of its voyage, now it reveals itself, now it illuminates the twenty bygone years it mutely lived with one. It could not say so much if it had not been there mutely the whole time, and what idiot would dare to assert that the same things had always been in it.

Elias Canetti, *The Human Province* (1943).

A book, like a person, has its fortunes with one; is lucky or unlucky in the precise moment of its falling in our way, and often by some happy accident counts with us for something more than its independent value.

Walter Pater, *Marius the Epicurean* (1885).

In a library we are surrounded by many hundreds of dear friends, but they are imprisoned by an enchanter in these paper and leathern boxes; and though they know us, and have been waiting two, ten, or twenty centuries for us – some of them – and are eager to give us a sign, and unbosom themselves, it is the law of their limbo that they must not speak until spoken to; and as the enchanter has dressed them, like battalions of infantry, in coat and jacket of one cut, by the thousand and ten thousand, your chance of hitting on the right one is to be computed by the arithmetical rule of Permutation and Combination – and not a choice out of three caskets, but out of half a million caskets all alike. But it happens in our experience, that in this lottery there are at least fifty or a hundred blanks to a prize.

Ralph Waldo Emerson, 'Books' (1860).

*****

I am not at all afraid of urging overmuch the propriety of frequent, very frequent, reading of the same book. The book remains the same, but the reader changes.

Matthew Browne, 'On the forming of opinions on books' (1866).

Still, it pulls us up short to come on writing we once thought splendid – *crucial* – and find it dull, badly dated, silly even. A measure of our growth maybe, but unsettling, too. Who were we when we raved about *this*?

David Long, 'On rereading' (1987).

I hate to read new books. There are twenty or thirty volumes that I have read over and over again, and these are the only ones that I have any desire ever to read at all. . . . When I take up a work that I have read before (the oftener the better) I know what I have to expect. The satisfaction is not

lessened by being anticipated. When the entertainment is altogether new, I sit down to it as I should to a strange dish, – turn
and pick out a bit here and there, and am in doubt what to
think of the composition. . . .

Besides, in thus turning to a well-known author, there is not
only an assurance that my time will not be thrown away, or my
palate nauseated with the most insipid or vilest trash, – but I
shake hands with, and look an old, tried, and valued friend in
the face, – compare notes, and chat the hours away. It is true, we
form dear friendships with such ideal guests – dearer, alas! and
more lasting, than those with our most intimate acquaintance.

William Hazlitt, 'On reading old books' (1817).

Contemporary books do not keep. The quality in them which
makes for their success is the first to go; they turn over night.

Cyril Connolly, *Enemies of Promise* (1938).

*****

One is always free to stop and read a book of a different
quality or an opposed opinion. A book doesn't trap a reader,
it is there to be taken or left.

John Updike, 'I was a teen-age library user'.

I also hate books that can be put down; and if they have no
narrative to sustain them then they had better, so far as I am concerned, be bloody good in other directions. Narrative is my
second connective principle in choice of reading. I have an
unlimited greed for it, which seriously distorts my literary judgement. An abysmally low boredom threshold has prevented me
from ever finishing countless serious and worthy novels by
serious and worthy authors. I can admire people like Richardson and George Eliot, but I could never read them for pleasure.

John Fowles, 'Of memoirs and magpies' (1975).

I remember well more than one summery occasion when my increasingly tired-looking Modern Library edition of Sterne's facetious, mind-addling classic was hauled down from its shelf into the sun and shade; once I took it with me to a week alone on Martha's Vineyard, thinking to force the issue. Alas, even the boredom of utter solitude was no match for the boredom that poured in waves off the chirpy pages of this particular great book. I made it as far as page 428, a half-faded book-mark tells me; but, like Scott on his return from the South Pole, I did not quite have the stuff to complete the job. I should have eaten the sledge dogs, like Amundsen.

John Updike, in *New York Times Book Review* (1991).

I myself have for many years kept beside my pallet Kant's *Critique of Pure Reason*. I have never got through it. I always begin again at the same place, to wit, the first line. The result is that I probably know the first three pages as well as any man alive, and that I am totally ignorant as to what comes after. I may say in self-defence that I am not in the least degree curious about what comes after; but there it is.

J. C. Squire, 'Reading in bed' (1927).

Sartor Resartus is simply unreadable, and for me that always sort of spoils a book.

Will Cuppy, *The Decline and Fall of Practically Everybody* (1950).

* * * * *

. . . once or twice she had peeped into the book her sister was reading, but it had no pictures or conversations in it, 'and what is the use of a book', thought Alice, 'without pictures or conversations?'

Lewis Carroll, *Alice in Wonderland* (1865).

* * * * *

The main point, therefore, about reading is to read. The first thing to do is to make absolutely sure that you really do like reading. The thing is supposed to be, and often is, a pleasure: there is no possible reason why it should be elevated into a duty. You should begin by reading ill-written books and those which your more literate friends decry. Well-written books often require some effort on the part of the reader, and, if you are only just beginning, this effort is a sheer waste of time. The test of whether you honestly enjoy reading is a simple one. If you leave your home and take your own book with you, it means that you are one of those who read sincerely. If, on the other hand, when you leave your home you rely either on the railway bookstall or on the books which you may, or may not, find there when you arrive, it means that you do not care for reading. If you belong to the latter class, all that I advise is never in any circumstances to discuss literature.

Harold Nicolson, 'How to read books' (1937).

Cultivate above all things a taste for reading. There is no pleasure so cheap, so innocent, and so remunerative as the real, hearty pleasure and taste for reading. It does not come to every one naturally. Some people take to it naturally, and others do not; but I advise you to cultivate it, and endeavour to promote it in your minds. In order to do that you should read what amuses you and pleases you. You should not begin with difficult works, because, if you do, you will find the pursuit dry and tiresome. I would even say to you, read novels, read frivolous books, read anything that will amuse you and give you a taste for reading.

Robert Lowe, 'Speech to the students of the Croydon Science and Art Schools' (1869).

A man ought to read just as inclination leads him; for what he reads as a task will do him little good.

Samuel Johnson, quoted in James Boswell, *Life of Johnson* (1791)

* * * * *

Once upon a time everybody recognised that print was a form of frozen sound, and reading then a form of listening. Today, with our over-developed ocular skill, we see a sentence, even a paragraph, at a glance and hear nothing at all. We read so fast that if our reading were still listening we should be hearing every word in that sentence or paragraph at once, or so nearly simultaneously that all the sounds would be telescoped together. Even if we heard them in their right order it would be like listening to a gramophone record spinning at some thousands of revolutions a minute. We should put our fingers in our ears to save them from so horrible a noise.

. . . It is hardest for those who have read voraciously in youth. Long before they have reached middle age, even if they neglect newspapers, they have acquired a habit of galloping through books, and become aware that, though, perhaps, they read more than ever, they get less from their reading than they did.

Arthur Ransome, 'On reading too fast' (1929).

. . . read your book, somewhat more slowly than modern educationalists recommend. Remember, you are trying to find out what the book has to say. You are not straining to reach the end, in order that you may read something else. If you don't like the book, you do not have to read it. Put it aside and read something you do like, because there is no reason at all why you should read what bores you during your serious reading time. You have to read enough boring stuff in the

ordinary way of life, without extending the borders of ennui.
But if you do like the book, if it engages you seriously, do not
rush at it. Read it at the pace at which you can pronounce and
hear every word in your own head. Read eloquently.

I know this is heresy. People who teach reading are dead
against what they call 'verbalizing'. If you verbalize, you lose
time. What time are they talking about? Time is one of the
great hobgoblins of our day. There is really no time except the
single, fleeting moment that slips by us like water, and to talk
about losing time, or saving time, is often a very dubious
argument. When you are reading you cannot save time, but
you can diminish your pleasure by trying to do so. What are
you going to do with this time when you have saved it? Have
you anything to do more important than reading? You are
reading for pleasure, you see, and pleasure is very important.

Robertson Davies, 'Reading' (1990).

We get no good
By being ungenerous, even to a book,
And calculating profits – so much help
By so much reading. It is rather when
We gloriously forget ourselves, and plunge
Soul-forward, headlong, into a book's profound,
Impassioned for its beauty and salt of truth –
'Tis then we get the right good from a book.

Elizabeth Barrett Browning, *Aurora Leigh* (1856).

* * * * *

However, many books,
Wise men have said, are wearisome; who reads
Incessantly, and to his reading brings not
A spirit and judgement equal or superior,
(And what he brings what needs he elsewhere seek?)

Uncertain and unsettled still remains,
Deep-versed in books and shallow in himself,
Crude or intoxicate, collecting toys
And trifles for choice matters, worth a sponge,
As children gathering pebbles on the shore.

John Milton, *Paradise Regained* (1671).

Read not to contradict and confute; nor to believe and take for granted; nor to find talk and discourse; but to weigh and consider. Some books are to be tasted, others to be swallowed, and some few to be chewed and digested; that is, some books are to be read only in parts; others to be read, but not curiously; and some few to be read wholly, and, with diligence and attention. Some books also may be read by deputy, and extracts made of them by others; but that would be only in the less important arguments, and the meaner sort of books; else distilled books are like common distilled waters, flashy things.

Francis Bacon, 'Of studies' (1625).

The art of skipping is, in a word, the art of noting and shunning that which is bad, or frivolous, or misleading, or unsuitable for one's individual needs. If you are convinced that the book or the chapter is bad, you cannot drop it too quickly. If it is simply idle and foolish, put it away on that account, – unless you are properly seeking amusement from idleness and frivolity.

Charles F. Richardson, *The Choice of Books* (1881).

As to collectors, it is quite true that they do not in general read their books successively straight through, and the practice of desultory reading, as it is sometimes termed, must be treated as part of their case, and if a failing, one cognate with their habit of collecting. They are notoriously addicted to the practice of standing arrested on some round of a ladder, where, having mounted up for some certain books, they have by wayward chance fallen upon another, in which, at the first opening, has come up a passage which fascinates the finder as the eye of the Ancient Mariner fascinated the wedding-guest, and compels him to stand there poised on his uneasy perch and read. Peradventure the matter so perused suggests another passage in some other volume which it will be satisfactory and interesting to find, and so another and another search is made, while the hours pass by unnoticed, and the day seems all too short for the pursuit which is a luxury and an enjoyment, at the same time that it fills the mind with varied knowledge and wisdom.

John Hill Burton, *The Book-Hunter* (1862).

10. 'CREATING A FRISSON': REVIEWERS AND REVIEWING

A critic is a man whom God created to praise greater men than himself, but who, by a curious blindness, has never been able to find them.

Richard Le Gallienne, *Retrospective Reviews: A Literary Log* (1896).

* * * * *

We admire the acuteness of the critic who reveals the unsuspected excellence of our favourite writer . . . But the rub comes when the judgement of the critic disagrees with ours. We discover that his laws have no penalties, and that if we get more enjoyment from breaking than from obeying, then we are just that much ahead. As for giving up an author just because the judgement of the critic is against him, who ever heard of such a thing? The staunchest canons of criticism are exploded by a genuine burst of enthusiasm.

Samuel McChord Crothers, *The Gentle Reader* (1906).

I have no intention of imitating those critics whose method of creating a *frisson* is to select the most distinguished author or artist and then, not call him bad, but imply that he is already recognised as bad by some unnamed and therefore awe-inspiring coterie. They do not write 'Mr Hardy is a bungler,' but: 'Unless Mr Jugg takes more pains, his work will soon be indistinguishable from Mr Hardy's.'

Gilbert Norwood, 'Too many books' (1926).

There are days when a reviewer approximates more and more to that robot figure on Brighton pier, who wheedles the passers-by in a brassy subhuman voice, and when they put down a coin hands out a cardboard square of commonplace and irrelevant criticism.

Cyril Connolly, 'Reviewers' (1938).

If you are a practised reviewer of fiction, you will very soon learn to divide the books you have to review into quite a few categories according to their subjects. Thus, they may deal with Family Life, Village Life, London Life, Married Life, Individual Life, School Life, American Life, Corpses, International Conspiracies, South Sea Islands, or Love. As you will not wish to read the books, I will set down a few hints as to what to say of each class. Family Life and Village Life are both rather sad, disagreeable subjects. The people who live in families and villages are seldom good or at all nice to one another. Villagers are the worst, for they are imbecile as well as criminal. They go further than families, as families only think and speak criminally, and villagers act. You may safely call a Village Life novel realistic and powerful, even, in some cases, sordid. If you call a Family Life novel any of these, you will probably be going further than the text warrants, and may be sued for libel. London Life novels are much gayer. They deal, as a rule, with London W. 1. You may say, if you like, that they are about well-known society figures, many of whom will be easily recognisable to their friends and enemies. London Life novels are not realistic, powerful, or sordid, as people in London have a wider range of entertainment and are therefore more cheerful. Besides, novels about persons who pay income tax are not realistic. And persons who pay super-tax are not considered by most reviewers real people at all. Novels about Married Life are often 'poignant studies of a very modern problem' (à propos, you will find much of what you need to say kindly supplied for you by the publisher on the paper wrapper. But you must not trust blurb-writers too implicitly, for they have not, any more than you, read the book about which they blurb) . . . Stories of School Life are a little *passé* now. But, should one come your way, you can safely say that it deals once more with the problems of adolescence from a realistic angle, and that nothing is shirked, though Mr – is always restrained.

American Life may be divided into sub-sections. There are novels about Eastern America, or civilised life (perhaps by Mrs Wharton or Miss Sedgwick), Middle Western Life (which you should praise), Wild Western Life (which are about cow-boys or long white trails, and published by Messrs. Hodder and Stoughton), and South American Life (which I recommend you to read, as they are probably readable).

Novels about Corpses are often readable, too. For the corpse, you should look in the library, in one of the early chapters, and there you will find the murdered body of an elderly gentleman. It is safe to say of this book that the mystery is well kept to the end (or else you spotted the murderer straight off, according as you wish well or ill to the author) and that there is a happy affair between the detective, or the suspected but innocent young man (you had better ascertain which) and the corpse's niece, daughter, or ward (you need not ascertain which).

Novels about International Conspiracies deal with Bolshevists, and relate world-wide schemes for the overthrow of established governments and the setting up of a world dominion. You will quite soon see if a book is about this. You may safely say that the Bolshevists are bad men, and that their schemes are defeated by the intrepid hero.

Books about South Sea Islands reveal themselves at once. If you open them anywhere, you will see 'yam,' 'bread-fruit,' 'palm toddy,' 'kanaka,' 'beach-comber,' or 'lagoon.' You can call them picturesque, romantic, or exciting, or (if you feel more like it) 'cheap lagoonery.'

Books about Love deal with a well-worn subject in a new and moving way.

Some reviewers like to be quoted by publishers in advertisements; others are shy, and do not. If you do, you should make your favourable comments detachable from the context; thus, if you desire to express distaste and yet be quoted, you may say 'This cannot be called a really good book,' and trust that the publishers may know which words to select. If you do *not* like being quoted, you should be careful to express any favourable views you may hold in a delicate and obscure way which shall elude the publisher's grasp, and see you do not hang your laudations like cullable blossoms on a bough.

Rose Macaulay, A Casual Commentary (1925).

The main function [of the basic OK critical phrases] is to imply that you, the critic, are an extraordinarily nice chap. Eg

OK *critical lines*

1. 'Thank goodness, there's no mention of Freud' OR 'Personally I'm sick of the Oedipus complex' (there need not, of course, be any reference to Freud or complexes in the work concerned).

2. 'Delightfully fresh and spontaneous'.

Both 1. and 2. will suggest that the critic, in spite of his rather scruffy appearance, *is himself pretty fresh and spontaneous.*

3. 'A rewarding experience'. ('Rewarding' is the new ok word for 1952. 'Climate of thought' is ok, but only just. 'Rebarbative' is *finito*.)

OK *attacks*

4. 'Personally I found the love-scenes rather embarrassing.'
5. 'There is a certain archness which I found displeasing.'

4. and 5. mean *'Though sensitive and cultured, my peasant stock ensures that I am ok for passion.'*

6. Quote misquotations of commas.

7. Complainingly quote clichés, or at any rate say, 'Why must "blood" always be "congealed"?' as if it *was* a cliché.

8. In criticizing any translation, take any five lines of the translation and then quote the original and say, 'Why not let's have the original, so much more force and point, etc.' If the original language is Syriac, so much the less chance of argument.

Stephen Potter, 'Litmanship' (1952)

. . . the prolonged, indiscriminate reviewing of books is a quite exceptionally thankless, irritating and exhausting job. It not only involves praising trash . . . but constantly *inventing* reactions towards books about which one has no spontaneous feelings whatever.

George Orwell, 'Confessions of a book reviewer' (1946).

I never read a book before reviewing it; it prejudices a man so.

Sydney Smith, quoted in H. Pearson, *The Smith of Smiths* (1934).

Attacking bad books is not only a waste of time but also bad for the character. If I find a book really bad, the only interest I can derive from writing about it has to come from myself, from such display of intelligence, wit and malice as I can contrive. One cannot review a bad book without showing off.

W. H. Auden, 'Reading' (1963).

It is a fine and splendid thing to have a critical mind so long as it doesn't take you so far that you can see nothing on every side of you for dust and ashes; the fact remains, however, that on looking around you it is the books that you have loved that count, not the books that you have criticised.

Hugh Walpole, *These Diversions: Reading* (1926).

11. 'THE SIGHT OF PRINT MADE HIM FEEL SICK': ENEMIES OF BOOKS

NATHANIEL

Sir, he hath never fed of the dainties that are bred in a book;
He hath not eat paper, as it were; he hath not drunk ink; his
intellect is not replenished; he is only an animal, only sensible in the duller parts.

William Shakespeare, *Love's Labour's Lost* (1598).

Joe never read. He was one of those boys who can go
through years of schooling and at the end of it are unable to
read ten lines consecutively. The sight of print made him feel
sick. I've seen him pick up one of my numbers of *Chums*, read
a paragraph or two and then turn away with just the same
movement of disgust as a horse when it smells stale hay.

George Orwell, *Coming up for Air* (1939).

Carol drove through an astonishing number of books from the
public library and from city shops. Kennicott was at first uncomfortable over her disconcerting habit of buying them. A book was
a book, and if you had several thousand of them right here in the
library, free, why the dickens should you spend your good
money? After worrying about it for two or three years, he decided
that this was one of the Funny Ideas which she had caught as a
librarian and from which she would never entirely recover.

Sinclair Lewis, *Main Street: The Story of Carol Kennicott* (1920).

'The Library? – I don't intend to have one,' was the answer. 'I
consider the private library an exploded superstition. We have
an excellent public library in the town, to which I make a point

of subscribing liberally. Mudie sends us fifteen new books every week, and if I want to make anything like a study of a subject it is open to me to run up to London and spend a few days at the British Museum. To my mind, our modern civilization shows few more satisfactory symptoms than the tendency of the public library everywhere to displace the private one. It is good, every way. The presence in a dwelling-house of a large collection of old books is extremely detrimental to health. Not only do they gather dust and so become nests for the breeding of fevers, but I am competently informed that the old leather of their bindings emits an odour that is directly productive of phthisis. I believe that, in nine cases out of ten, the family library is at the root of the consumption that carries off the children of the house. I am so firmly persuaded of this that nothing will ever induce me to stay with people who use their book-room for a general sitting-room. I would as soon dine with the skeleton in the cupboard, or sleep in the family vault.'

Mary Elizabeth Christie, 'Recollections of my grandfather's library' (1898).

I do not like books. I believe I have the smallest library of any literary man in London, and I have no wish to increase it. I keep my books at the British Museum and at Mudie's, and it makes me very angry if anyone gives me one for my private library. I once heard two ladies disputing in a railway carriage as to whether one of them had or had not been wasting money. 'I spent it in books,' said the accused, 'and it's not wasting money to buy books.' 'Indeed, my dear, I think it is,' was the rejoinder, and in practice I agree with it. Webster's Dictionary, Whitaker's Almanack, and Bradshaw's Railway Guide should be sufficient for any ordinary library; it will be time enough to go beyond these when the mass of useful and entertaining matter which they provide has been mastered.

Samuel Butler, 'Ramblings in Cheapside' (1890)

The few books we owned were largely reference books, bought by subscription through magazines: *Enquire Within*, *What Everyone Wants to Know* and, with its illustrations of a specimen man and woman (minus private parts and pubic hair), *Everybody's Home Doctor*. No book, whether from the library or otherwise, was ever on view. Anthony Powell's 'Books do furnish a room' was not my mother's way of thinking. 'Books untidy a room' more like, or, as she would have said, 'Books upset.' So if there were any books being read they would be kept out of sight, generally in the cabinet that had once held a wind-up gramophone, bought when they were first married and setting up house.

Alan Bennett, 'The treachery of books' (1990).

The bookcase doubled as a drinks cabinet. Or perhaps that should be the other way around. Three glass decanters with silver labels hanging around their necks boasted Brandy, Whisky and Port, though I had never known anything in them, not even at Christmas. Dad's whisky came from a bottle, Dimple Haig, that he kept in a hidden cupboard at the back of the bookcase where he also kept his Canada Dry and a jar of maraschino cherries for when we all had snowballs at Christmas. The front of the drinks cabinet housed his entire collection of books.

The family's somewhat diminutive library had leatherette binding and bore Reader's Digest or The Folio Society on their spines. Most were in mint condition, and invariably 'condensed' or 'abridged'. Six or so of the books were kept in the cupboard at the back, with the Dimple Haig and a bottle of advocaat: a collection of stories by Edgar Allan Poe, a dog-eared Raymond Chandler, a Philip Roth and a neat pile of *National Geographics*. There was also a copy of Marguerite Patten's *All Colour Cookbook*.

It was a tight fit in between the wall and the back of the bookcase. Dad just opened the door and leaned in to get his whisky; it was more difficult for me to get round there, to wriggle into a position where I could squat in secret and turn the pages of the hidden books. I don't know how Marguerite Patten would feel knowing that she was kept in the same cupboard as *Portnoy's Complaint*, or that I would flip excitedly from one to the other. I hope my father never sells them. 'For sale, one copy each of Marguerite Patten's *All Colour Cookery* and Philip Roth's *Portnoy's Complaint*, first edition, d/w, slightly stained.'

Nigel Slater, *Toast: The Story of a Boy's Hunger* (2003).

*****

He had instructed his secretary to furnish the library, and she had bought books by the yard and sent them to be bound to the height of the shelves, so that the titles at the page-tops were in many cases trimmed, and sometimes even the first lines were missing.

Alberto Manguel, *A History of Reading* (1996).

Around the hall and in a small gallery were the books, arranged in carved oaken cases. They consisted principally of old polemical writers, and were much more worn by time than use. In the centre of the library was a solitary table with two or three books on it, an inkstand without ink, and a few pens parched by long disuse. The place seemed fitted for quiet study and profound meditation. It was buried deep among the massive walls of the abbey, and shut up from the tumult of the world. I could only hear now and then the shouts of the school-boys faintly swelling from the cloisters, and the sound of a bell tolling for prayers, echoing soberly along the roofs of the abbey. By degrees the shouts of merriment grew fainter and fainter, and at length died away; the bell ceased to toll, and a profound silence reigned through the dusky hall.

I had taken down a little thick quarto, curiously bound in parchment, with brass clasps, and seated myself at the table in a venerable elbow-chair. Instead of reading, however, I was beguiled by the solemn monastic air, and lifeless quiet of the place, into a train of musing. As I looked around upon the old volumes in their mouldering covers, thus arranged on the shelves, and apparently never disturbed in their repose, I could not but consider the library a kind of literary catacomb, where authors, like mummies, are piously entombed, and left to blacken and moulder in dusty oblivion. . . .

While I sat half murmuring, half meditating these unprofitable speculations with my head resting on my hand, I was thrumming with the other hand upon the quarto, until I accidentally loosened the clasps; when, to my utter astonishment, the little book gave two or three yawns, like one awakening from a deep sleep; then a husky hem; and at length began to talk. At first its voice was very hoarse and broken, being much troubled by a cobweb which some studious spider had woven across it; and having probably contracted a cold from long exposure to the chills and damps of the abbey. In a short time, however, it became more distinct, and I soon found it an exceedingly fluent conversable little tome. Its language, to be sure, was rather quaint and obsolete, and its pronunciation, what, in the present day, would be deemed barbarous; but I shall endeavour, as far as I am able, to render it in modern parlance.

It began with railings about the neglect of the world – about merit being suffered to languish in obscurity, and other such commonplace topics of literary repining, and complained bitterly that it had not been opened for more than two centuries. That the dean only looked now and then into the library, sometimes took down a volume or two, trifled with them for a few moments, and then returned them to their shelves. 'What a plague do they mean,' said the little quarto, which I began to perceive was somewhat choleric, 'what a plague do they mean by keeping several thousand volumes of us shut up here, and watched by a set of old vergers, like so many beauties in a harem, merely to be looked at now and then by the dean? Books were written to give pleasure and to be enjoyed; and I would have a rule passed that the dean should pay each of us a visit at least once a year; or if he is not equal to the task, let them once in a while turn loose the whole school of Westminster among us, that at any rate we may now and then have an airing.'

'Softly, my worthy friend,' replied I, 'you are not aware how much better you are off than most books of your generation. By being stored away in this ancient library, you are like the treasured remains of those saints and monarchs, which lie enshrined in the adjoining chapels; while the remains of your contemporary mortals, left to the ordinary course of nature, have long since returned to dust.'

'Sir,' said the little tome, ruffling his leaves and looking big, 'I was written for all the world, not for the bookworms of an abbey. I was intended to circulate from hand to hand, like other great contemporary works, but here have I been clasped up for more than two centuries, and might have silently fallen a prey to these worms that are playing the very vengeance with my intestines, if you had not by chance given me an opportunity of uttering a few last words before I go to pieces.'

Washington Irving, 'The mutability of literature' (1820–1).

*****

It was some time before Adam could get attended to.

'I've nothing but some very old clothes and some books,' he said.

But here he showed himself deficient in tact, for the man's casual air disappeared in a flash.

'Books, eh?' he said. 'And what sort of books, may I ask?'

'Look for yourself.'

'Thank *you*, that's what I mean to do. *Books*, indeed.'

Adam wearily unstrapped and unlocked his suitcase.

'Yes,' said the Customs officer, menacingly, as though his worst suspicions had been confirmed, 'I should just about say you had got some books.'

One by one he took the books out and piled them on the counter. A copy of Dante excited his especial disgust.

'French, eh?' he said. 'I guessed as much, and pretty dirty, too, I shouldn't wonder. Now just you wait while I look up these here *books*' – how he said it! – 'in my list. Particularly against books the Home Secretary is. If we can't stamp out literature in the country, we can at least stop its being brought in from outside. That's what he said the other day in Parliament, and I says, 'Hear, hear . . .' . . .

With the help of a printed list (which began 'Aristotle, Works of (Illustrated)' they went through Adam's books, laboriously, one at a time, spelling out the titles. . . .

'Well, see here,' he said, 'you can take these books on architecture and the dictionary, and I don't mind stretching a point for once and letting you have the history books, too. But this book on Economics comes under Subversive Propaganda. That you leaves behind. And this here *Purgatorio* doesn't look right to me, so that stays behind, pending enquiries.'

Evelyn Waugh, *Vile Bodies* (1930).

SID

Good is it?

HANCOCK

Good? This is red hot this is mate. I'd hate to think of a book like this getting into the wrong hands. As soon as I've finished this I shall recommend they ban it.

Alan Simpson and Ray Galton, *Hancock's Half Hour: The Missing Page* (1960).

*****

Mr Birdsall, of Northampton, sent Mr Blades, in 1879, by post, a fat little worm he had found in an old volume. Mr Blades did all, and more than all, that could be expected of a humane man to keep the creature alive, actually feeding him with fragments of Caxtons and seventeenth-century litera- ture; but it availed not, for in three weeks the thing died, and as a result of a post-mortem was declared to be *Æcopheria pseudotretella*.

Augustine Birrell, 'Bookworms' (1906).

*****

But it is not always easy to destroy books. They may not have as many lives as a cat, but they certainly die hard; and it is sometimes difficult to find a scaffold for them. This diffi- culty once brought me almost within the Shadow of the Rope. I was living in a small and (as Shakespeare would say) heaven-kissing flat in Chelsea, and books of inferior minor verse gradually accumulated there until at last I was faced with the alternative of either evicting the books or else leaving them in sole, undisturbed tenancy and taking rooms else- where for myself. Now, no one would have bought these books. I therefore had to throw them away or wipe them off the map altogether. But how? There were scores of them. I had no kitchen range, and I could not toast them on the gas- cooker or consume them leaf by leaf in my small study fire – for it is almost as hopeless to try to burn a book without opening it as to try to burn a piece of granite. I had no dust- bin; my debris went down a kind of flue behind the staircase, with small trap-doors opening to the landings. The difficulty with this was that the larger books might choke it; the authorities, in fact, had labelled it 'Dust and Ashes Only'; and in any case I did not want to leave the books intact, and some dustman's unfortunate family to get a false idea of English poetry from them. So in the end I determined to do to them what so many people do to the kittens; tie them up and consign them to the river. I improvised a sack, stuffed the books into it, put it over my shoulder, and went down the stairs into the darkness.

It was nearly midnight as I stepped into the street. There was a cold nip in the air; the sky was full of stars; and the greenish-yellow lamps threw long gleams across the smooth, hard road. Few people were about; under the trees at the corner a Guardsman was bidding a robust goodnight to his girl, and here and there rang out the steps of solitary travellers making their way home across the bridge to Battersea. I turned up my overcoat collar, settled my sack comfortably across my shoulders, and strode off towards the little square glow of the coffee-stall which marked the near end of the bridge, whose sweeping iron girders were just visible against the dark sky behind. A few doors down I passed a policeman who was flashing his lantern on the catches of basement windows. He turned. I fancied he looked suspicious, and I trembled slightly. The thought occurred to me: 'Perhaps he suspects I have swag in this sack.' I was not seriously disturbed, as I knew that I could bear investigation, and that nobody would be suspected of having stolen such goods (though they *were* all first editions) as I was carrying. Nevertheless I could not help the slight unease which comes to all who are eyed suspiciously by the police, and to all who are detected in any deliberately furtive act, however harmless. He acquitted me, apparently; and, with a step that, making an effort, I prevented from growing more rapid, I walked on until I reached the Embankment.

It was then that all the implications of my act revealed

themselves. I leaned against the parapet and looked down into the faintly luminous swirls of the river. Suddenly I heard a step near me; quite automatically I sprang back from the wall and began walking on with, I fervently hoped, an air of rumination and unconcern. The pedestrian came by me without looking at me. It was a tramp, who had other things to think about; and, calling myself an ass, I stopped again. 'Now's for it,' I thought; but just as I was preparing to cast my books upon the waters I heard another step – a slow and measured one. The next thought came like a blaze of terrible blue lightening across my brain: 'What about the splash?' A man leaning at midnight over the Embankment wall: a sudden fling of his arms: a great splash in the water. Surely, and not without reason, whoever was within sight and hearing (and there always seemed to be some one near) would at once rush at me and seize me. In all probability they would think it was a baby. What on earth would be the good of telling a London constable that I had come out into the cold and stolen down alone to the river to get rid of a pack of poetry? I could almost hear his gruff, sneering laugh: 'You tell that to the Marines, my son!'

So for I do not know how long I strayed up and down, increasingly fearful of being watched, summoning up my courage to take the plunge and quailing from it at the last moment. At last I did it. In the middle of Chelsea Bridge there are projecting circular bays with seats in them. In an agony of decision I left the Embankment and hastened straight for the first of these. When I reached it I knelt on the seat. Looking over, I hesitated again. But I had reached the turning-point. 'What!' I thought savagely, 'under the resolute mask that you show your friends is there really a shrinking and contemptible coward? If you fail now, you must never hold your head up again. Anyhow, what if you *are* hanged for it? Good God! you worm, better men than you have gone to the gallows!'

With the courage of despair I took a heave. The sack dropped sheer. A vast splash. Then silence fell again. No one came. I turned home; and as I walked I thought a little sadly of all those books falling into that cold torrent, settling slowly down through the pitchy dark, and subsiding at last on the ooze of the bottom, there to lie forlorn and forgotten whilst the unconscious world of men went on.

Horrible bad books, poor innocent books, you are lying there still; covered, perhaps, with mud by this time, with only a stray rag of sacking sticking out of the slime into the opaque brown tides. Odes to Diana, Sonnets to Ethel, Dramas on the Love of Lancelot, Stanzas on a First Glimpse of Venice, you lie there in a living death, and your fate is perhaps worse than you deserved. I was harsh with you. I am sorry I did it.

J. C. Squire, 'On destroying books' (1927).

. . . the size of the unread mass has positive and evil effects. In the honest it causes worry, and a sense of waste; in the dishonest it causes snobbery and the desire to outshine. There is but one remedy: a wholesale destruction. Quite nine-tenths of the good books should be burnt. . . . There remains the chief and most arduous task, to decide which books already extant should perish. The work is enormous, and must be spread over many years. Ten thousand *per annum* seems a likely figure, which could be rapidly increased as the public grew accustomed to the system and observed that the sky did not fall. . . . any of these ten thousand may be saved if it can be shown that the public really wishes to save it. The proof must, however, be given in deeds, not words as heretofore and should be conducted on the following lines. The list is promulgated on January 1st, but the destruction does not begin until August 1st. During July all publishers and librarians are to make a return of the number of persons who during the preceding six months have purchased or read each of the books proscribed. Anyone claiming to have read a book owned by himself would be subject to a brief oral examination. The works would then be arranged in three categories. Any which had been read by ten thousand people should be struck from the list and given immunity for fifteen years. Those which had been read by less than ten but more than five thousand should be immune for five years. Each work which had found less than five thousand supporters should be retained for one year if any single person could be found to prove his love for it by making a sacrifice to ensure its preservation. This would form the sound test of that 'revelling in' authors of which we hear so much. The sacrifices demanded would, of course, vary according to the original support. A book with four thousand adherents would escape if £100 were paid into the Treasury; the rescue of one with only a thousand would mean fifty years' penal servitude – often a mere bagatelle if all the essayists and editors contributed. At the end of the scale books with less than ten readers could survive if one person consented to go on the scaffold. The executions would take place on August 15th in public, and it would be an uplifting sight when some grey-haired fanatic passed into the Beyond crying, 'Long live *Butterflies of North-East Bucks!*' Nor would this heroism be needed in the following year for the same work. Such a public confession would kindle popular curiosity, and the book might easily leap into the fifteen-year class. We should have great families in which it was the tradition for the eldest son to give up his young life for some Portuguese grammar or volume of *vers libre* which his forbears had protected from the committee for centuries.

Gilbert Norwood, 'Too many books' (1926).

It was a flaking three-storey house in the ancient part of the city, a century old if it was a day, but like all houses it had been given a thin fireproof plastic sheath many years ago, and this preservative shell seemed to be the only thing holding it in the sky.

'Here we are!'

The engine slammed to a stop. Beatty, Stoneman, and Black ran up the sidewalk, suddenly odious and fat in the plump fireproof slickers. Montag followed.

They crashed the front door and grabbed at a woman, though she was not running, she was not trying to escape. She was only standing, weaving from side to side, her eyes fixed upon a nothingness in the wall as if they had struck her a terrible blow upon the head. Her tongue was moving in her mouth, and her eyes seemed to be trying to remember something, and then they remembered and her tongue moved again:

'"Play the man, Master Ridley; we shall this day light such a candle, by God's grace, in England, as I trust shall never be put out."'

'Enough of that!' said Beatty. 'Where are they?'

He slapped her face with amazing objectivity and repeated the question. The old woman's eyes came to a focus upon Beatty. 'You know where they are or you wouldn't be here,' she said.

Stoneman held out the telephone alarm card with the complaint signed in telephone duplicate on the back:

'Have reason to suspect attic; 11 No. Elm, City. E.B.'

'That would be Mrs Blake, my neighbour,' said the woman, reading the initials.

'All right men, let's get 'em!'

Next thing they were up in musty blackness, swinging

silver hatchets at doors that were, after all, unlocked, tumbling through like boys all rollick and shout. 'Hey!' A fountain of books sprang down upon Montag as he climbed shuddering up the sheer stair-well . . .

Books bombarded his shoulders, his arms, his upturned face. A book alighted, almost obediently, like a white pigeon, in his hands, wings fluttering. In the dim, wavering light, a page hung open and it was like a snowy feather, the words delicately painted thereon. In all the rush and fervour, Montag had only an instant to read a line, but it blazed in his mind for the next minute as if stamped there with fiery steel. 'Time has fallen asleep in the afternoon sunshine.' He dropped the book. Immediately, another fell into his arms.

'Montag, up here!'

Montag's hand closed like a mouth, crushed the book with wild devotion, with an insanity of mindlessness to his chest. The men above were hurling shovelfuls of magazines into the dusty air. They fell like slaughtered birds and the woman stood below, like a small girl, among the bodies.

Montag had done nothing. His hand had done it all, his hand, with a brain of its own, with a conscience and a curiosity in each trembling finger, had turned thief. Now it plunged the book back under his arm, pressed it tight to sweating armpit, rushed out empty, with a magician's flourish! Look here! Innocent! Look!

He gazed, shaken, at that white hand. He held it way out, as if he were far-sighted. He held it close, as if he were blind.

'Montag!'

He jerked about.

'Don't stand there, idiot!'

The books lay about like great mounds of fishes left to dry. The men danced and slipped and fell over them. Titles glittered their golden eyes, falling, gone.

'Kerosene!'

They pumped the cold fluid from the numbered 451 tanks strapped to their shoulders. They coated each book, they pumped rooms full of it.

They hurried downstairs, Montag staggered after them in the kerosene fumes.

'Come on, woman!'

The woman knelt among the books, touching the drenched leather and cardboard, reading the gilt titles with her fingers while her eyes accused Montag.

'You can't ever have my books,' she said.

'You know the law,' said Beatty. 'Where's your common sense? None of these books agree with each other. You've been locked up here for years with a regular damned Tower of Babel. Snap out of it! The people in these books never lived. Come on now!'

She shook her head . . . She opened the fingers of one hand slightly and in the palm of the hand was a single slender object.

An ordinary kitchen match.

Ray Bradbury, Fahrenheit 451 (1953).

Personally, I am dead against the burning of books.

Augustine Birrell, 'Bookworms' (1906).

There are probably false impressions abroad as to the susceptibility of literature to destruction by fire. Books are not good fuel, as, fortunately, many a housemaid has found, when, among other frantic efforts and failures in fire-lighting, she has reasoned from the false data of inflammability of a piece of paper. In the days when heretic books were burned, it was necessary to place them on large wooden stages, and after all the pains taken to demolish them, considerable readable masses were sometimes found in the embers; whence it was supposed that the devil, conversant in fire and its effects, gave them his special protection. In the end it was found easier and cheaper to burn the heretics themselves than their books.

John Hill Burton, *The Book-Hunter* (1862).

* * * * *

Sir Everard had never been himself a student, and . . . held the common doctrine, that idleness is incompatible with reading of any kind, and that the mere tracing the alphabetical characters with the eye is in itself a useful and meritorious task, without scrupulously considering what ideas or doctrines they may happen to convey.

Walter Scott, *Waverley* (1814).

12. INVOLVING 'MOST OF THE DEADLY SINS': BOOKISH VICES

He who loves to commune with books is led to detest all manner of vice.

Richard de Bury, *Philobiblon* (1599).

'Ay, indeed,' said another book-stall keeper, 'anything scarce or curious, when it's an old book, is kept out of the streets; if it's not particularly decent sir,' (with a grin), 'why it's reckoned all the more curious, – that's the word, sir, I know, "curious". I can tell how many beans make five as well as you or anybody. Why, now, there's a second-hand bookseller not a hundred miles from Holborn – and a pleasant, nice man he is, and does a respectable business – and he puts to the end of his catalogue – they all have catalogues that's in a good way – two pages that he calls "Facetiae". They're titles and prices of queer old books in old language – indecent books, indeed. He sends his catalogues to many clergymen and learned people; and to any that he thinks wouldn't much admire seeing his "Facetiae", he pulls the last leaf out, and sends his catalogue, looking finished without it. Those last two pages aren't at all the worst part of his trade among buyers that's worth the money.'

Henry Mayhew, 'Of the character of books of the street-sale' (1861–2).

* * * * *

Over the last ten years or so, I have managed not to finish certain books. With barely a twinge of conscience, I hurl down what bores me or doesn't give what I crave: ecstasy, transcendence, a thrill of mysterious connection. For, more than anything else, readers are thrill-seekers, though I don't read thrillers, not the kind sold under that label anyway. They don't thrill; only language thrills.

Lynne Sharon Schwartz, *Ruined by Reading* (1996).

It would be wrong to think that because I read books, any books, some over and over, I enjoyed them. I did not read for pleasure; I was an addict. I read for greed. I jammed books into my brain like a compulsive eater glutting herself, gobbling up one book so that I could gobble up another. My reading was mostly displacement activity; when other children were playing, or getting exercise, training in some sport or hanging out with their mates, I was reading. The only alternative was a boredom so heavy and slow that it squashed my soul flat.

Germaine Greer, in *The Pleasure of Reading* (1992).

To a considerable extent reading has become, for almost all of us, an addiction, like cigarette-smoking. We read, most of the time, not because we wish to instruct ourselves, not because we long to have our feelings touched and our imagination fired, but because reading is one of our bad habits, because we suffer when we have time to spare and no printed matter with which to plug the void.

Aldous Huxley, 'Writers and readers' (1936).

Some people read for instruction, which is praiseworthy, and some for pleasure, which is innocent, but not a few read from habit, and I suppose that this is neither innocent nor praiseworthy. Of that lamentable company am I. Conversation after a time bores me, games tire me, and my own thoughts, which we are told are the unfailing resource of a sensible man, have a tendency to run dry. Then I fly to my book as the opium-smoker to his pipe. I would sooner read the catalogue of the Army and Navy Stores or Bradshaw's Guide than nothing at all, and indeed I have spent many delightful hours over both these works. At one time I never went out without a second-hand bookseller's list in my pocket. I know no reading more fruity. Of course to read in this way is as reprehensible as doping, and I never cease to wonder at the impertinence of great readers who, because they are such, look down on the illiterate. From the stand-point of what eternity is it better to have read a thousand books than to have ploughed a million furrows? Let us admit that reading with us is just a drug that we cannot do without – who of this band does not know the restlessness that attacks him when he has been severed from reading too long, the apprehension and irritability, and the sigh of relief which the sight of a printed page extracts from him? – and so let us be no more vainglorious than the poor slaves of the hypodermic needle or the pint-pot.

W. Somerset Maugham, 'The book bag' (1951).

It seems doubtful whether the habitual reader can ever be cured. Tell him that reading is the last resort of the intellectu-ally destitute, he merely laughs. His book-sodden mind is unable to respond to the strongest admonition. It is impossi-ble, he says, for him to give up reading.

Obviously it is not impossible. As Mark Twain said of smoking, I have given it up scores of times. For hours at a stretch. I could do it again, no doubt. . . .

[If] you are determined to cut down your reading it is best not to start too ambitiously. You may think it easy enough to drop your daily paper, but the very first morning, in bus, train or tube, you find that you are left with nothing better to

occupy you than the observation of your fellow creatures –
and even that is difficult: they are hidden behind newspapers.
When I have embarked on a course of this kind of fasting it
has had a corrupting influence. I have surprised myself cheat-
ing – reading the paper of the man next or opposite to me.
Whenever I have come out without a book in my pocket I
have been put to the expense of buying one before I have got
through the day.

On the whole, perhaps the best thing to do is to give up the
idea of giving up reading.

Daniel George, 'The reading habit' (1954).

* * * * *

Apparently, there is a skill that people pay to acquire called
speed reading. This makes as much sense as a course in speed
love-making.

Guy Browning, 'How to . . . read', *The Guardian Weekend Magazine*,

5 April, 2003.

* * * * *

I want to read you some new passages from an interleaved
copy of my book. You haven't read the printed part yet. I gave
you a copy of it, but nobody reads a book that is given to him.
Of course not. Nobody but a fool expects him to. He reads a
little in it here and there, perhaps, and he cuts all the leaves if
he cares enough about the writer, who will be sure to call on
him some day, and if he is left alone in his library for five
minutes will have hunted every corner of it until he has found
the book he sent – if it is to be found at all, which doesn't
always happen, if there's a penal colony anywhere in a garret
or closet for typographical offenders and vagrants.

Oliver Wendell Holmes, *The Poet at the Breakfast Table* (1872).

* * * * *

To be proud of having two thousand books would be absurd. You might as well be proud of having two top-coats. After your first two thousand difficulty begins, but until you have ten thousand volumes the less you say about your library the better. *Then* you may begin to speak.

Augustine Birrell, 'Book buying' (1905)

I should never call myself a book lover, any more than a people lover: it all depends on what's inside them. Nor am I a book collector: when a don asked me how many books I had, I really couldn't reply, but this didn't matter as all he wanted to tell me was that he had 25,000, or 50,000, or some improbable number. I was too polite to deliver a variant of Samuel Butler's 'I keep my books round the corner, in the British Museum', yet at the same time I felt a wave of pity, as if he had confessed to kleptomania or some other minor psychological compulsion.

Philip Larkin, 'Books' (1972).

To possess few books, and those not too rich and rare for daily use, has this advantage, that the possessor can make himself master of them all, can recollect their peculiarities, and often remind himself of their contents. The man that has two or three thousand books can be familiar with them all; he that has thirty thousand can hardly have a speaking acquaintance with more than a few.

Edmund Gosse, *Gossip in a Library* (1891).

* * * * *

Nearly all bookish people are snobs, and especially the more enlightened among them. They are apt to assume that if a writer has immense circulation, if he is enjoyed by plain persons, and if he can fill several theatres at once, he cannot possibly be worth reading and merits only indifference and disdain.

Arnold Bennett, 'I read a "thriller" – and startle my friends' (1928).

He that will have no books but those that are scarce, evinces about as correct a taste in literature, as he would do in friendship, who would have no friends but those whom all the rest of the world have sent to coventry.

Charles Colton, *Lacon* (1820).

* * * * *

A 'bestseller' is a celebrity among books. It is a book known primarily (sometimes exclusively) for its well-knownness.

Daniel Boorstin, *The Image* (1962).

. . . the books that are talked about can be talked about just as well without being read.

Samuel McChord Crothers, *The Gentle Reader* (1906).

Pride of reading is a terrible thing. There are certain literary sets in which the book is an instrument of tyranny. If you have not read it, you are made to feel unspeakably abject, for the book you have not read is always the one book in the world you should have read. It is the sole test of literary insight, good taste, and mental worth. To confess that you have not read it is to expose yourself as an illiterate person. It is like admitting that you have never eaten with a fork. Now, when this social pressure is brought to bear upon a man, what happens? This depends on his moral character. If there is a flaw in it anywhere, it breaks down. Weak, sensitive persons will invariably stammer out a lie. The temptation to escape the ignominy is irresistible. The have-reads are hard, insolent and cruelly triumphant. The haven't-reads feel that they must either tell lies or slink away. Then there are all sorts of miserable compromises. Without actually saying that he has read one of the obligatory books, a weak character will act as if he had. He ventures a few of those vague, universal comments which he knows are bound to be true of anything, anywhere. But it is a wretched piece of business, and most harrowing to the nerves. The awful fidgetiness of a poor baited unread man, when he thinks he is being cornered, is pitiful to see.

Next comes the stage of involuntary deceit. By talking about books as if he had read them he comes to think that he has. He uses third-hand quotations as if they were his own. At this point humbug enters the heart; the mind, as you might say, becomes encrusted with its own pretence. Finally, there is literary second childishness, oblivion, and death. Some choose the more virtuous course by reading books just to say they have read them, thereby saving their souls, perhaps, but certainly swamping their intellects.

Frank Moore Colby, 'The books I haven't read' (1926).

* * * * *

Some read to think – these are rare; some to write, these are common; and some read to talk, and these form the great majority. The first page of an author not unfrequently suffices all purpose of this latter class, of whom it has been said, that they treat books as some do lords; they inform themselves of their *titles*, and then boast of an intimate acquaintance.

Charles Colton, *Lacon* (1820).

There are two motives for reading a book: one, that you enjoy it; the other, that you can boast about it.

Bertrand Russell, *The Conquest of Happiness* (1930).

If by chance one happened actually to have read a book on the morning of publication, Coad could always go one better. I have myself rushed round to Coad with a copy of, say, T. D. Pontefract's *The Tea Party* at 11 o' clock – two hours after it was issued – to see if I could for once be one up on him over a new book. I do not remember what he said, but experience has taught me it must have been either (a) 'Let me lend you the American edition. It's beautifully printed and hasn't got that stupid cut on page 163,' or (b) (more simply) 'Good old Pontefract – still churning them out.'

This answer (b) brings me to the second sub-qualification which made things more possible for Coad in his pursuit of Keeping Abreastmanship. There are latest books and latest books, he would imply; and after he reached the age of forty-four, when reading became even more difficult for him, he would make a tremendous point, though as up to date as ever, of only buying the books 'which interested him.'

'Look, I've got a prize,' he would say to me. 'I've got it too,' said I breathlessly, pointing to my new Julius Simon.

'Ah, good, good,' Coad says now. 'But I didn't actually mean that one. Where does the Mysterious Religious Character come in this time? Chapter XIV?'

This maddened me, (a) because I had in fact been rather moved by Chapter XIV, and (b) because I knew Coad was going to pull out some small, almost privately printed book and say, 'I meant this – John's new book on the architecture of lift shafts. It's most frightfully good.'

Stephen Potter, 'Litmanship' (1952).

Of course it can be argued that reading too much is just as pernicious as reading too little. I can recall from my undergraduate days a girl who used to moan, when she was slightly drunk: 'I've read everything on the Senior English course lists, and where has it got me?' What she meant was that her reading had not provided her with beauty, or charm, or sexual irresistibility. That girl had gobbled eight plays of Shakespeare, a play by Ben Jonson, all of *Pamela*, the whole eight volumes of *Clarissa*, eight novels by Dickens, one by Thackeray, one by Trollope, a large wodge of Henry James, a substantial vegetarian mass of Bernard Shaw and God knows what else, and at the end of it all her mind was as flat as Holland. All she had gained were thick glasses and bad breath, doubtless the result of literary constipation.

Robertson Davies, 'Reading' (1990).

*****

Then there is the question of foreign literature. That is a terrible question, and one which is safer to avoid. I knew a woman once, she was a German woman, and she spoke French like M. Claudel, and English almost as excellently as I do myself. She also knew Italian and was excessively tiresome about the early poetry of, . . . well let us say Leopardi. Then one day she asked me about Sologub. I said I had read some stories of his which had much impressed me. She asked me whether I had read them in Russian. I said that I had read them in English.

'Oh,' she answered, sinking back among the cushions, 'I think it is a crime to read the Russian masters except in the original.'

Harold Nicolson, 'How to read' (1937).

My abstracts of each book were made in the French language: my observations often branched into particular essays; and I can still read, without contempt, a dissertation of eight folio pages on eight lines (287–294) of the fourth *Georgic* of Virgil.

Edward Gibbon, *Autobiography of Edward Gibbon* (1796).

I turn down the upper corner for page-marking and the lower corner to identify passages I want to xerox for my commonplace book.

Anne Fadiman, *Ex Libris: Confessions of a Common Reader* (1998).

*****

I believe that when it comes to books, conventional morality doesn't exist.

Arturo Pérez-Reverte, *The Dumas Club* (1993).

Thomas Blinton was a book-hunter . . . His 'harmless taste' really involved most of the deadly sins, or at all events a fair working majority of them. He coveted his neighbours' books. When he got the chance he bought books in a cheap market and sold them in a dear market, thereby degrading literature to the level of trade. He took advantage of the ignorance of uneducated persons who kept book-stalls. He was envious, and grudged the good fortune of others, while he rejoiced in their failures. He turned a deaf ear to the appeals of poverty. He was luxurious, and laid out more money than he should have done on his selfish pleasures, often adorning a volume with morocco binding when Mrs Blinton sighed in vain for some old *point d'Alençon* lace. Greedy, proud, envious, stingy, extravagant, and sharp in his dealings, Blinton was guilty of most of the sins which the Church recognises as 'deadly'.

Andrew Lang, *Books and Bookmen* (1913).

She began to saunter about the room, examining the book-shelves between the puffs of her cigarette-smoke. Some of the volumes had the ripe tints of good tooling and old morocco, and her eyes lingered on them caressingly, not with the appreciation of the expert, but with the pleasure in agreeable tones and textures that was one of her inmost susceptibilities. Suddenly her expression changed from desultory enjoyment to active conjecture, and she turned to Seldon with a question.

'You collect, don't you – you know about first editions and things?'

'As much as a man may who has no money to spend. Now and then I pick up something in the rubbish heap; and I go and look on at the big sales.'

She had again addressed herself to the shelves, but her eyes now swept them inattentively, and he saw that she was preoccupied with a new idea.

'And Americana – do you collect Americana?'

Seldon stared and laughed.

'No, that's rather out of my line. I'm not really a collector, you see; I simply like to have good editions of the books I am fond of.'

She made a slight grimace. 'And Americana are horribly dull, I suppose?'

'I should fancy so – except to the historian. But your real collector values a thing for its rarity. I don't suppose the buyers of Americana sit up reading them all night – old Jefferson Gryce certainly didn't.'

She was listening with keen attention. 'And yet they fetch fabulous prices, don't they? It seems so odd to want to pay a lot for an ugly badly-printed book that one is never going to read! And I suppose most of the owners of Americana are not historians either?'

'No; very few of the historians can afford to buy them. They have to use those in the public libraries or in private collections.

It seems to be the mere rarity that attracts the average collector.'

He had seated himself on an arm of the chair near which she was standing, and she continued to question him, asking which were the rarest volumes, whether the Jefferson Gryce collection was really considered the finest in the world, and what was the largest collection in the world, and what was the largest price ever fetched by a single volume.

It was so pleasant to sit there looking up at her, as she lifted now one book and then another from the shelves, fluttering the pages between her fingers, while her drooping profile was outlined against the warm background of old bindings, that he talked on without pausing to wonder at her sudden interest in so un-suggestive a subject. But he could never be long with her without trying to find a reason for what she was doing, and as she replaced his first edition of La Bruyère and turned away from the bookcases, he began to ask himself what she had been driving at. Her next question was not of a nature to enlighten him. She paused before him with a smile which seemed at once designed to admit him to her familiarity, and to remind him of the restrictions it imposed.

'Don't you ever mind,' she asked suddenly, 'not being rich enough to buy all the books you want?'

Edith Wharton, *The House of Mirth* (1905).

*****

My Aunt Carol . . . places reproductions of Audubon paintings horizontally to mark the exact paragraph where she left off. If the colored side is up, she was reading the left-hand page; if it's down, the right-hand page. A college classmate of mine, a lawyer, uses his business cards, spurning his wife's silver Tiffany bookmarks because they are a few microns too thick and may leave vestigial stigmata.

Anne Fadiman, *Ex Libris: Confessions of a Common Reader* (1998).

This collection had cost him a considerable sum of money. He would not suffer, in his library, the books he liked to resemble other similar volumes, printed on cotton paper with the watermarks of *Auvergne*.

Formerly in Paris he had ordered made, for himself alone certain volumes which specially engaged mechanics printed from hand presses. Sometimes, he applied to Perrin of Lyons, whose graceful, clear type was suitable for archaic reprints of old books. At other times he dispatched orders to England or to America for the execution of modern literature and works of the present century. Still again, he applied to a house in Lille, which for centuries had possessed a complete set of Gothic characters; he also would send requisitions of the old Enschede printing house of Haarlem whose foundry still has the stamps and dies of certain antique letters.

He had followed the same method in selecting his papers. Finally growing weary of the snowy Chinese and the nacreous and gilded Japanese papers, the white Whatmans, the brown Hollands, the buff-coloured Turkeys and Seychal Mills, and equally disgusted with all mechanically manufactured sheets, he had ordered special laid paper in the mould, from the old plans of Vire which still employ the pestles once in use to grind hemp. To introduce a certain variety into his collection, he had repeatedly brought from London prepared stuffs, paper interwoven with hairs, and as a mark of his distain for bibliophiles, he had a Lubeck merchant prepare for him an improved candle paper of bottle-blue tint, clear and somewhat brittle, in the pulp of which the straw was replaced by golden spangles resembling those which dot Danzig brandy.

Under these circumstances he had succeeded in procuring unique books, adopting obsolete formats which he had bound by Lortic, by Trautz, by Bauzonnet or Chambolle, by the successors of Cape, in irreproachable covers of old silk, stamped cow hide, Cape goat skin, in full bindings with compartments and in mosaic designs, protected by tabby or moiré watered silk, ecclesiastically ornamented with clasps and corners, and sometimes even enamelled by Gruel Engelmann with silver oxide and clear enamels.

Thus, with the marvellous Episcopal lettering used in the old house of Le Clere, he had Baudelaire's works printed in a large format recalling that of ancient missals, on a very light and spongy Japan paper, soft as elder pith and imperceptibly tinted with a light rose hue through its milky white. This edition, limited to one copy, printed with a velvety black Chinese ink, had been covered outside and then recovered within with a wonderful genuine sow skin, chosen among a thousand, the colour of flesh, its surface spotted where the hairs had been and adorned with black silk stamped in cold iron in miraculous designs by a great artist.

That day, Des Esseintes took this incomparable book from his shelves and handled it devotedly, once more reading certain pieces which seemed to him, in this simple but inestimable frame, more than ordinarily penetrating.

J.-K. Huysmans, *Against the Grain* (1884).

Clark, an investment analyst, won't let his wife raise the blinds until sundown, lest the bindings fade. He buys at least two copies of his favourite books, so that only one need be subjected to the stress of having its pages turned. When his visiting mother-in-law made the mistake of taking a book off the shelf, Clark shadowed her around the apartment to make sure she didn't do anything unspeakable to it – such as placing it facedown on a table.

Anne Fadiman, *Ex Libris: Confessions of a Common Reader* (1998).

'Why, you see, sir, no man can comfortably do without three copies of a book. One he must have for a show copy, and he will probably keep it at his country-house; another he will require for his own use and reference; and unless he is inclined to part with this, which is very inconvenient, or risk the injury of his best copy, he must needs have a third at the service of his friends.'

John Hill Burton, *The Book-Hunter* (1862).

* * * * *

Books are good enough in their own way, but they are a mighty bloodless substitute for life. It seems a pity to sit like the Lady of Shalott, peering into a mirror, with your back turned on all the bustle and glamour of reality.

R. L. Stevenson, 'An apology for idlers' (1881).

Someone reading a book is likely to be living a far more exciting life on the page than in reality. One of the things you don't find characters in books doing is sitting down and reading a book for a couple of hours. Especially in thrillers.

Guy Browning, 'How to . . . read', *The Guardian Weekend Magazine*,

5 April, 2003.

13. 'CONSTRUCTING GATES AND DRAWBRIDGES': THINGS TO DO WITH BOOKS

When I was four, I liked to build castles with my father's pocket-sized, twenty-two-volume set of Trollope. My brother and I had a set of wooden blocks as well, but the Trollopes were superior: midnight blue, proportioned to fit a child's hand, and, because they were so much thinner than they were tall, perfect, as cards are, for constructing gates and drawbridges.

Anne Fadiman, *Ex Libris: Confessions of a Common Reader* (1998).

I should explain that I cannot write unless I have a sloping desk, and the reading-room of the British Museum, where alone I can compose freely, is unprovided with sloping desks. Like every other organism, if I cannot get exactly what I want I make shift with the next thing to it; true, there are no desks in the reading-room, but, as I once heard a visitor from the country say, 'it contains a large number of very interesting works.' I know it was not right, and hope the Museum authorities will not be severe upon me if any of them reads this confession; but I wanted a desk, and set myself to consider which of the many very interesting works which a grateful nation places at the disposal of its would-be authors was best suited for the purpose.

For mere reading I suppose one book is pretty much as good as another: but the choice of a desk-book is a more serious matter. It must be neither too thick nor too thin; it must be large enough to make a substantial support; it must be strongly bound so as not to yield or give; it must not be too troublesome to carry backwards and forwards; and it must live on shelf C, D, or E, so that there need be no stooping or reaching too high . . .

For weeks I made experiments upon sundry poetical and philosophical works, whose names I have forgotten, but could not succeed in finding my ideal desk, until at length, more by luck than cunning, I happened to light upon Frost's *Lives of Eminent Christians*, which I had no sooner tried than I discovered it to be the very perfection and *ne plus ultra* of everything that a book should be. It lived in Case No. 2008, and I accordingly took at once to sitting in Row B, where for the last dozen years or so I have sat ever since.

The first thing I have done whenever I went to the Museum has been to take down Frost's *Lives of Eminent Christians* and carry it to my seat. It is not the custom of modern writers to refer to the works to which they are most deeply indebted, and I have never, that I remember, mentioned it by name before; but it is to this book alone that I have looked for support during many years of literary labour, and it is round this to me invaluable volume that all my own have, page by page, grown up. There is none in the Museum to which I have been under anything like such constant obligation, none which I can so ill spare, and none which I would choose so readily if I were allowed to select one single volume and keep it for my own.

On finding myself asked for a contribution to *The Universal Review*, I went, as I have explained, to the Museum, and presently repaired to bookcase No. 2008 to get my favourite volume. Alas! it was in the room no longer. It was not in use, for its place was filled up already; besides, no one ever used it but myself. . . . Till I have found a substitute I can write no more, and I do not know how to find even a tolerable one. I should try a volume of Migne's *Complete Course of Patrology*, but I do not like books in more than one volume, for the volumes vary in thickness, and one never can remember which one took; the four volumes, however, of Bede in Giles's *Anglican Fathers* are not open to this objection, and I have reserved them for favourable consideration. Mather's *Magnalia* might do, but the binding does not please me; Cureton's *Corpus Ignatianum* might also do if it were not too thin. I do not like taking Norton's *Genuineness of the Gospels*, as it is just possible some one may be wanting to know whether the Gospels are genuine or not, and be unable to find out because I have got Mr Norton's book. Baxter's *Church History of England*, Lingard's *Anglo-Saxon Church*, and Cardwell's *Documentary Annals*, though none of them as good as Frost, are works of considerable merit; but on the whole I think Arvine's *Cyclopaedia of Moral and Religious Anecdote* is perhaps the one book in the room which comes within measurable distance of Frost. . . . Some successor I must find, or I must give up writing altogether, and this I should be sorry to do.

Samuel Butler, 'Quis desiderio' (1888).

*****

I've had a notion of writing a murder mystery in which a book was the weapon. It always seemed to me the greatest loss of the game Clue[do] that one could never do it to Colonel Mustard, in the library, with the *book*.

Matthew Battles, *Library: An Unquiet History* (2003).

Books of poems lying around are handy
For killing persistent irritating flies

Geoffrey Grigson, 'For liquid flies' (1980).

*****

By the time Charles had settled himself comfortably in the carriage, spreading out on the table in front of him a bar of Cadbury's milk chocolate, his ticket, two apples and a paperback edition of *Great Expectations*, the 9.15 from London to Bristol was already moving out of the station. . . . He looked around with satisfaction at the other people in the carriage, then he tore a small piece from a page of *Great Expectations*, rolled it into a ball and popped it into his mouth. This was an old habit of his: he could not resist eating books.

. . . 'Would you like some? It's delicious.' He offered the book to Philip, who gracefully declined.

Peter Ackroyd, *Chatterton* (1987)

When my son was eight months old, it could truthfully be said that he devoured literature. Presented with a book, he chewed it. A bit of Henry's DNA has been permanently incorporated into the warped pages of *Goodnight Moon*, and the missing corners of pages 3 and 8 suggest that a bit of *Goodnight Moon* has been permanently incorporated into Henry. He was, of course, not the first child to indulge in bibliophagy. The great Philadelphia bookdealer A. S. W. Rosenbach deduced that one reason first editions of *Alice in Wonderland* were so scarce was that so many of them had been eaten.

Anne Fadiman, *Ex Libris: Confessions of a Common Reader* (1998).

* * * * *

'He sentenced me, as I said, to two months' P.C.T.F.O., and I was marched off and put in chokey. I got the same scoff as you, of course, and an hour's exercise a day; but they only changed our books three times a week, I'd have gone barmy.'

'What did you read?' I asked him.

'Well, I got some Hugh Walpole. The others couldn't read

it. I slipped one in to them, and they said it was a lot of bal-locks about old parsons and their wives, but I read them, and liked them.'

'He'd be a good man and you in chokey all right,' said I, 'and Galsworthy. When I was in Walton I got a bloody great book of his, *The Forsyte Saga*. When I was starving with hunger, and perished with the cold in the old flowery dell all alone, it was like having a feed of plum pudding and port wine.'

'Did you know,' said Joe, 'there's a book called *Crime and Punishment* – it's about a geezer that kills an 'ore with an 'atchet.'

'It's by a Russian called Dostoyevsky,' said I. 'Did you read it?'

'No,' said Joe, 'can't say as I did. But I 'eard a bloke tell it once. You know the way you tell a film. It was double good. But the best book I ever saw in the nick was the Bible. When I was in Brixton on remand, I 'ad one in the flowery. Smashing thin paper for rolling dog-ends in. I must 'ave smoked my way through the book of Genesis, before I went to court.'

Brendan Behan, *Borstal Boy* (1958).

For one [book] that is read from start to finish, thousands are leafed through, other thousands lie motionless, others are jammed against mouseholes, thrown at rats, others are stood on, sat on, drummed on, have gingerbread baked on them or are used to light pipes.

Georg Christoph Lichtenberg, *Aphorisms* (c.1765–99).

A big leather-bound volume makes an ideal razorstrap. A thin book is useful to stick under a table with a broken caster to steady it. A large, flat atlas can be used to cover a window with a broken pane. And a thick, old-fashioned heavy book with a clasp is the finest thing in the world to throw at a noisy cat.

Mark Twain, apocryphal.

* * * * *

The father of a friend of mine used to find that breathing in the atmosphere of a well-stocked secondhand bookshop – the mustier the better – was a certain cure for his acute constipation. A bowl of All-Bran just doesn't offer the same satisfaction as a good shelf of old Everyman's Library volumes.

James Carter, 'Notes and Queries', *The Guardian.*

I knew a gentleman, who was so good a manager of his time, that he would not even lose that small proportion of it which the calls of nature obliged him to pass in the neces-sary-house, but gradually went through all the Latin poets in those moments. He bought, for example, a common edition of Horace, of which he tore off gradually a couple of pages, carried them with him to that necessary place, read them first, and then sent them down as a sacrifice to Cloacina; this was so much time fairly gained; and I recommend to you to follow his example. It is better than only doing what you cannot help doing at those moments; and it will make any book which you shall read in that manner, very present to your mind.

Lord Chesterfield, letter to his son, 11 December, 1747.

The bugs are much better now, but they still don't give us any Jeyes paper in the lavatory. I have worked my way steadily through a whole copy of Jung's *Psychology of the Unconscious* in the last few weeks with the result that there is hardly a WC in the house which is not 'hors de combat'.

Joan Wyndham, *Love is Blue: A Wartime Diary*, 14 May, 1941.

* * * * *

'I've been drunk for about a week now, and I thought it might sober me up to sit in a library.'

'Has it?'

'A little bit, I think. I can't tell yet. I've only been here an hour.'

F. Scott Fitzgerald, The Great Gatsby (1925).

. . . Clio [the Muse of History] could at least refrain from reading the works which, by a legal fiction, she was supposed to inspire. Once or twice in the course of a century, she would glance into this or that new history book, only to lay it down with a shrug of her shoulders. Some of the mediaeval chronicles she rather liked. But when, one day, Pallas asked her what she thought of 'The Decline and Fall of the Roman Empire' her only answer was . . . For people who like that kind of thing, that is the kind of thing they like. This she did let slip. Generally, throughout all the centuries, she kept up a pretence of thinking history was the greatest of the arts. She always held her head high among her Sisters. It was only on the sly that she was an omnivorous reader of dramatic and lyric poetry. She watched with keen interest the early developments of the prose romance in southern Europe; and after the publication of 'Clarissa Harlow' she spent practically all her time reading novels. It was not until the Spring of the year 1863 that an entirely new element forced itself into her peaceful life. Zeus fell in love with her.

To us, for whom so quickly, 'time doth transfix the flourish set on youth,' there is something strange, even a trifle ludicrous, in the thought that Zeus, after all these years, is still at the beck and call of his passions. And it seems anyhow lamentable that he has not yet gained self-confidence enough to appear in his own person to the lady of his choice, and is still at pains to transform himself into whatever object he deems likeliest to please her. To Clio, suddenly from Olympus, he flashed down in the semblance of Kinglake's 'Invasion of the Crimea' (four vols., large 8vo, half-calf). She saw though his disguise immediately, and, with great courage and independence, bade him begone. Rebuffed, he was not deflected. Indeed it would seem that Clio's high spirit did but sharpen his desire. Hardly a day passed but he appeared in a recently discovered fragment of Polybius, an advance copy of the forthcoming issue of 'The Historical Review', the note-book of Professor Carl Vörtschlaffen . . . One day, all-prying Hermes told him of Clio's secret addiction to novel-reading. Thenceforth, year in, year out, it was in the form of fiction that Zeus wooed her. The sole result was that she grew sick of the sight of novels, and found a perverse pleasure in reading history.

Max Beerbohm, *Zuleika Dobson* (1911).

14. 'A HOLE WHERE A BOOK OUGHT TO BE': LOSS

There are many horrible sights in the multiverse. Somehow, though, to a soul attuned to the subtle rhythms of a library, there are few worse sights than a hole where a book ought to be.

Terry Pratchett, *Guards! Guards!* (1989).

For, if you wish to keep books, you must guard them against young dogs as well as against borrowers and furniture removers. It was a collie six months old that ate my first copy of 'Pride and Prejudice'.

Robert Lynd, 'Out of print' (1923).

A long day (it was in June) brought me to Richmond in the afternoon. Two pennyworth of bread and cheese and a pennyworth of small beer, which I had on the road, and one halfpenny that I had lost somehow or other, left three pence in my pocket. With this for my whole fortune, I was trudging through Richmond in my blue smock-frock and my red garters tied under my knees, when, staring about me, my eye fell upon a little book, in a bookseller's window: *Tale of a Tub*; price 3*d*. The title was so odd, that my curiosity was excited. I had the 3*d*., but, then, I could have no supper. In I went and got the little book, which I was so impatient to read, that I got over into a field, at the upper corner of Kew Gardens, where there stood a haystack. On the shady side of this, I sat down to read. The book was so different from anything that I had ever read before: it was something so new to my mind, that, though I could not at all understand some of it, it delighted me beyond description; and it produced what I have always considered a sort of birth of intellect. I read on till it was dark, without any thought about supper or bed. When I could see no longer, I put my little book in my pocket, and tumbled down by the side of the stack, where I slept till the birds in Kew Garden awaked me in the morning; when off I started to Kew, reading my little book. . . . The gardener, seeing me fond of books, lent me some gardening books to read; but, these I could not relish after my *Tale of a Tub*, which I carried about with me wherever I went, and when I, at about twenty years old, lost it in a box that fell overboard in the Bay of Funday in North America, the loss gave me greater pain than I have ever felt at losing thousands of pounds.

William Cobbett, *Autobiography* (1855).

*****

It happened to me last May to lose my home with all contents in a night of that phenomenon that we oddly called *Blitz* . . . [I]t destroyed my flat, leaving not a wrack behind, or, rather, nothing but wracks. Of furniture, books and pictures nothing stayed but a drift of loose, scorched pages fallen through three floors to street-level, and there lying sodden in a mass of wreckage smelling of mortality, to trouble me with hints of what had been. Here was a charred, curled page from one of the twelve volumes of the Oxford Dictionary, telling of hot-beds, hotch-pots, hot cockles, hotes and hotels; there, among a pile of damp ashes and smashed boards, were a few pages from Pepys, perhaps relating of another London fire, a few from Horace Walpole, urbane among earthquakes, revolutions and wars, knowing that all things pass. But no book remains; my library, with so many other libraries is gone.

When the first stunned sickness begins to lift a little, one perceives that something must be done about lost books. One makes lists; a prey to frenetic bibliomania, I made lists for weeks; when out, I climbed my ruins, seeking in vain; when in, I made lists. A list of the books I had had; that is the saddest list; perhaps one should not make it. A list of those one cannot hope (for one reason or another) to have again. A list of those that one hopes to replace one day, but not yet. Another of those to replace at once, directly one has shelves again – the indispensables. Another of the good riddances. One has, by inadvertence, all kinds of books; some are better gone; I had some like that, and they went.

Rose Macaulay, 'Losing one's books', *The Spectator*, 7 November, 1941.

Poking about in the rubble, I found at times scraps of parchment that had drifted down from the scriptorium and the library and had survived like treasures buried in the earth; I began to collect them, as if I were going to piece together the torn pages of a book. Then I noticed that in one of the towers there rose, tottering but still intact, a circular staircase to the scriptorium, and from there, by climbing a sloping bit of the ruin, I could reach the level of the library: which, however, was only a sort of gallery next to the outside walls, looking down into the void at every point.

Along one stretch of wall I found a bookcase, still miraculously erect, having come through the fire I cannot say how; it was rotted by water and consumed by termites. In it there were still a few pages. Other remnants I found by rummaging in the ruins below. Mine was a poor harvest, but I spent a whole day reaping it, as if from those disiecta membra of the library a message might reach me. Some fragments of the parchment had faded, others permitted the glimpse of an image's shadow, or the ghost of one or more words. At times I found pages where whole sentences were legible; more often,

intact bindings, protected by what had once been metal studs.
... Ghosts of books, apparently intact on the outside but consumed within; yet sometimes a half page had been saved, an
incipit was discernible, a title.

I collected every relic I could find, filling two travelling
sacks with them, abandoning things useful to me in order to
save that miserable hoard.

Along the return journey and afterward at Melk, I spent
many, many hours trying to decipher those remains. Often
from a word or a surviving image I could recognize what the
work had been. When I found, in time, other copies of those
books, I studied them with love, as if destiny had left me this
bequest, as if having identified the destroyed copy were a
clear sign from heaven that said to me: Tolle et lege. At the
end of my patient reconstruction, I had before me a kind of
lesser library, a symbol of the greater, vanished one: a library
made up of fragments, quotations, unfinished sentences,
amputated stumps of books.

Umberto Eco, *The Name of the Rose* (1983).

Books which he loved not only for their burden, but
intrinsically, for varying qualities of paper and print, kept
reminding him that they were no longer to be fingered and
read. Not only were the books lost and the thoughts in the
books, but what was to him, perhaps, the most searching
loss of all, the hours of rumination which lifted him above
himself and bore him upon their muffled and enormous
wings. Not a day passed but he was reminded of some single
volume, or of a series of works, whose very positions on the
walls was so clearly indented on his mind. He had taken
refuge from this raw emptiness in a superhuman effort to
concentrate his mind exclusively upon the string of ceremonies which he had daily to perform. He had not tried to
rescue a single volume from the shelves, for even while the

flames leapt around him he knew that every sentence that escaped the fire would be unreadable and bitter as gall, something to taunt him endlessly. It was better to have the cavity in his heart yawning and completely empty than mocked by a single volume.

Mervyn Peake, *Titus Groan* (1946).

15. 'AN INNOCENT AND BECOMING SPECTACLE': THE LANDSCAPE OF BOOKS

. . . books (you know those things that look like blocks but come apart on one side).

F. Scott Fitzgerald, letter to Zelda, 4 May, 1940.

There is no place, in which a man can move or sit, in which the outside of a book can be otherwise than an innocent and becoming spectacle.

Thomas Love Peacock, *Crotchet Castle* (1831).

When I go to libraries now I look at books as physical objects. I turn them around and check out the binding. One of the nice things about books is that they're private. You take a book home and you're free to experience it any way you want.

Aberlardo Morell, *A Camera in a Room: Photographs by Aberlardo Morell* (1995).

On a chance we tried an important-looking door, and walked into a high Gothic library, panelled with carved English oak, and probably transported complete from some ruin overseas.

A stout, middle-aged man, with enormous owl-eyed spectacles, was sitting somewhat drunk on the edge of a great table, staring with unsteady concentration at the shelves of books. As we entered he wheeled excitedly around and examined Jordan from head to foot.

'What do you think?' he demanded impetuously.

'About what?'

He waved his hand towards the book-shelves.

'About that. As a matter of fact you needn't bother to ascertain. I ascertained. They're real.'

'The books?'

He nodded.

'Absolutely real – have pages and everything. I thought they'd be nice durable cardboard. Matter of fact, they're absolutely real. Pages and – Here! Lemme show you.'

Taking our scepticism for granted, he rushed to the bookcases and returned with Volume One of the 'Stoddard Lectures'.

'See!' he cried triumphantly. 'It's a bona-fide piece of printed matter. It fooled me. This fella's a regular Belasco.'

F. Scott Fitzgerald, *The Great Gatsby* (1925).

To be strong-backed and neat-bound is the desideratum of a volume. Magnificence comes after.

Charles Lamb, 'Detached thoughts on books and reading' (1833).

Like Webster's *Dictionary*, we're Morocco-bound.

Frank Butler and Don Hartman, as sung by Bob Hope and Bing Crosby in *The Road to Morocco* (1942).

On another small table stood Zuleika's library. Both books were in covers of dull gold. On the back of one cover BRAD-SHAW, in beryls, was encrusted; on the back of the other, A.B.C. GUIDE, in amethysts, beryls, chrysoprases, and garnets.

Max Beerbohm, *Zuleika Dobson* (1911).

* * * * *

There is a kinde of Physiognomy in the Titles of Bookes no less than in the faces of men, by which a Skilful Observer will as well know what to expect from the one as the other.

Samuel Butler, *Prose Observations* (c.1660s).

The Newman arrived almost a week ago and I'm just beginning to recover. I keep it on the table with me all day, every now and then I stop typing and reach over and touch it. Not because it's a first edition; I just never saw a book so beautiful. I feel vaguely guilty about owning it. All that gleaming leather and gold stamping and beautiful type belongs in the pine-panelled library of an English country home; it wants to be read by the fire in a gentleman's leather easy chair – not on a second-hand studio couch in a one-room hovel in a broken-down brownstone front.

Helene Hanff, letter to Frank Doel, 15 October, 1950.

And see how it lies open anywhere! There isn't a book in my library that has such a generous way of laying its treasures before you. From Alpha to Omega, calm, assured rest at any page that your choice or accident may light on. No lifting of a rebellious leaf like an upstart servant that does not know his place and can never be taught manners, but tranquil, well-bred repose. A book may be a perfect gentleman in his aspect and demeanour, and this book would be good company for personages like Roger Ascham and his pupils the Lady Elizabeth and the Lady Jane Grey.

Oliver Wendell Holmes, *The Poet at the Breakfast Table* (1872).

And he became a connoisseur of paper-smells. He told Beharry, 'You know, I could just smell a book and tell how old it is.' He always held that the book with the best smell was the Harrap's French and English dictionary, a book he had bought, as he told Beharry, simply for the sake of its smell.

V. S. Naipaul, *The Mystic Masseur* (1957).

*****

There was a richness and mystery in the thick black type, a hint of bursting overflowing material in the serried lines and scant margin. To this day I am bored by the sight of widely spaced type, and a little islet of text in a sailless sea of white paper.

Edith Wharton, *A Backward Glance* (1934).

And he began to acquire some sensitivity to type-faces. Although he owned nearly every Penguin that had been issued he disliked them as books because they were mostly printed in Times, and he told Beharry that it looked cheap, 'like a paper'.

V. S. Naipaul, *The Mystic Masseur* (1957).

I remember well his getting those fat, shapeless, spongy German books, as if one would sink in them, and be bogged in their bibulous unsized paper; and watching him as he impatiently cut them up, and dived into them in his rapid, eclectic way, tasting them, and dropping for my play such a lot of soft, large, curled bits from the paper-cutter, leaving the edges all shaggy.

John Brown, 'Letter to John Cairns, D.D.' (1861).

*****

Books often differ, even if they're part of the same edition. No two books are the same really. From birth they all have distinguishing details. And each book lives a different life: it can lose pages, or have them added or replaced, or have a new binding . . . Over the years two books printed on the same press can end up looking entirely different.

Arturo Pérez-Reverte, *The Dumas Club* (1993).

Due attention to the inside of books, and due contempt for the outside, is the proper relation between a man of sense and his books.

Lord Chesterfield, letter to his son, 10 January, 1749.

Not everyone likes used books. The smears, smudges, underlinings, and ossified toast scintillae left by their previous owners may strike daintier readers as a little icky, like second-hand underwear. When I was young I liked my books young as well. Virginal paperbacks, their margins a tabula rasa for narcissistic scribbles, were cheap enough to inspire minimal guilt when I wrote in them and bland enough to accept my defacements without complaint. In those days, just as I believed that age would buffet other people's bodies but not my own, so I believed my paperbacks would last forever. I was wrong on both counts. My college Penguins now explode in clouds of acidic dust when they are prized from their shelves. *Penny Wise and Book Foolish*, on the other hand, remains ravishing at the age of sixty-eight, its binding still firm and its bottle-green cover only slightly faded.

Anne Fadiman, *Ex Libris: Confessions of a Common Reader* (1998).

As often as I survey my bookshelves I am reminded of Lamb's 'ragged veterans'. Not that all my volumes came from the second-hand stall; many of them were neat enough in new covers, some were even stately in fragrant bindings, when they passed into my hands. But so often have I removed, so rough has been the treatment of my little library at each change of place, and, to tell the truth, so little care have I given to its well-being at normal times (for in all practical matters I am idle and inept), that even the comeliest of my books show the results of unfair usage. More than one has been foully injured by a great nail driven into a packing-case – this but the extreme instance of the wrongs they have undergone. Now that I have leisure and peace of mind, I find myself growing more careful – an illustration of the great truth that virtue is made easy by circumstance. But I confess that, so long as a volume holds together, I am not much troubled as to its outer appearance.

I know men who say they had as lief read any book in a library copy as in one from their own shelf. To me that is unintelligible. For one thing, I know every book of mine by its *scent*, and I have but to put my nose between the pages to be reminded of all sorts of things. My Gibbon, for example, my well-bound eight-volume Milman edition, which I have read and read and read again for more than thirty years – never do I open it but the scent of the noble page restores to me all the exultant happiness of that moment when I received it as a prize. Or my Shakespeare, the Great Cambridge Shakespeare – it has an odour which carries me yet further back in life; for these volumes belonged to my father, and before I was old enough to read them with understanding, it was often permitted me, as a treat, to take down one of them from the bookcase, and reverently to turn the leaves. The volumes smell exactly as they did in that old time, and what a strange tenderness comes upon me when I hold one of them in my hand.

George Gissing, *The Private Papers of Henry Ryecroft* (1903).

A book is like a sandy path which keeps the indent of footsteps.

Graham Greene, *The Human Factor* (1978).

Some men live like moths in libraries, not being better for the books, but the books the worse for them, which they only soil with their fingers.

Thomas Fuller, *The History of the Worthies of England* (1662).

On a level with the eye, when sitting at the tea-table in my little cottage at Grasmere, stood the collective works of Edmund Burke. The book was to me an eye-sore and an ear-sore for many a year, in consequence of the cacophonous title lettered by the bookseller upon the back – 'Burke's Works'. . . . Wordsworth took down the volume; unfortunately it was uncut; fortunately, and by a special Providence as to him, it seemed, tea was proceeding at the time. Dry toast required butter; butter required knives; and knives then lay on the table; but sad it was for the virgin purity of Mr Burke's as yet unsunned pages, that every knife bore upon its blade testimonies of the service it had rendered. Did *that* stop Wordsworth? Did that cause him to call for another knife? Not at all; he

'Look'd at the knife that caus'd his pain:

And look'd and sigh'd, and look'd and sigh'd again';

and then, after this momentary tribute to regret, he tore his way into the heart of the volume with his knife, that left its greasy honours behind it upon every page: and are they not there to this day?

Thomas de Quincey, 'William Wordsworth and Robert Southey'
(1839).

. . . a book reads the better, which is our own, & has been so long known to us, that we know the topography of its blots, & dogears, and can trace the dirt in it to having read it at tea with buttered muffins, or over a pipe, which I think is the maximum.

Charles Lamb, letter to Samuel Taylor Coleridge, 11 October, 1802.

The book lay in her lap. She realised that for more than five minutes she had been looking at the porousness of the paper, the crease at the corner of page 17 which someone had folded over as a mark.

Michael Ondaatje, *The English Patient* (1992).

. . . my hands remembered the crazed and embossed leathers, corners eroded to board, paperbacks soft from the sea air. And slipped between the books, newspaper clippings fragile as mica.

Anne Michaels, *Fugitive Pieces* (1997).

Called on Miss Lamb. I looked over Lamb's library in part. He has the finest collection of shabby books I ever saw. Such a number of first-rate works of genius, but filthy copies, which a delicate man would really hesitate touching, is, I think, nowhere to be found.

Henry Crabb Robinson, diary entry for 10 January, 1834.

Every scholar should have a book infirmary attached to his library. There should find a peaceable refuge the many books, invalids from their birth, which are sent 'with the best regards of the Author'; the respected but unpresentable cripples which have lost a cover; the odd volumes of honoured sets which go mourning all their days for their lost brother; the school-books which have been so often the subjects of assault and battery, that they look as if the police-court must know them by heart; these and still more the pictured story-books, beginning with Mother Goose . . . will be precious mementos by-and-by, when children and grandchildren come along. What would I not give for that dear little paper-bound quarto, in large and most legible type, on certain pages of which the tender hand that was the shield of my infancy had crossed out with deep black marks something awful, probably about BEARS.

Oliver Wendell Holmes, *The Poet at the Breakfast Table* (1872).

* * * * *

In those days I could afford few books, certainly in hardback, and so wrote my name in them as I seldom do nowadays.

Alan Bennett, 'Austerity in colour' (2004).

I opened it at page 96 – the secret page on which I write my name to catch out borrowers and book-sharks.

Flann O'Brien, 'The forgetting of eaten bread'.

My father had a small library of a hundred or so, from which I tried a *Collected Writings of Victor Hugo*, mysteriously inscribed in my father's hand, 'G. M. Davenport, Apr. 24, 1934, Havana, Cuba,' where I am positive my father never set foot.

Guy Davenport, 'On reading' (1987).

Literature, as I saw it then, was a vast open range, my equivalent of the cowboy's dream. I felt free as any nomad to roam where I pleased, amid the wild growth of books. Eventually I formed my own book herds and brought them into more or less orderly systems of pasturage. I even branded them with a bookplate that had once been the family brand: a stirrup drawn simply and elegantly by my father.

Larry McMurtry, *Walter Benjamin at the Dairy Queen* (1999).

The outward and visible mark of the citizenship of the book-lover is his book-plate. There are many good bibliophiles who abide in the trenches, and never proclaim their loyalty by a book-plate. They are with us, but not of us; they lack the courage of their opinions; they collect with timidity or carelessness; they have no heed for the morrow. Such a man is liable to great temptations. He is brought face to face with that enemy of his species, the borrower, and dares not speak with him in the gate. If he had a book-plate he would say, 'Oh! certainly I will lend you this volume, if it has not my book-plate in it; of course, one makes a rule never to lend a book that has.' He would say this, and feign to look inside the volume, knowing right well that this safeguard against the borrower is there already. To have a book-plate gives a collector great serenity and self-confidence.

Edmund Gosse, *Gossip in a Library* (1891).

* * * * *

The practice attributed to the Chancellor of annotating his books is looked on by collectors as in the general case a crime which should be denied benefit of clergy.

John Hill Burton, *The Book-Hunter* (1862).

. . . it is an excellent habit to make pencil notes. These should be conducted on some system such as will demonstrate to subsequent readers of the book (of your copy of the book) how bright and studious you are.

The best thing to do is to scribble a sort of guide or index at the end of the book, which gives to your errant markings a certain conformity and meaning. This index, however, should be of a very personal nature, and not understandable to the uninitiate. My own books are scored with such annotations. I do not write 'very feeble and cheap' in the margin of a particular passage. I merely mark the thing with a neat but non-committal line against the side. And at the end I put 'F and C. pp. 23, 58, 69, 78, 92, 105, 114,' and so on. Nor do I confine myself to denigration. 'G.B.' I put, 'pp. 54, 98, 224, 669, 9956, 10456, 24378,' 'G.B.' means 'Good Bits,' just as 'B.B.' signifies 'Bad Bits' or 'l.o.s.o.p,' 'Lack of sense of proportion'.

Harold Nicolson, 'How to read books' (1937).

Why should a wealthy person . . . be put to the trouble of pretending to read at all? Why not a professional book-handler to go in and suitably maul his library for so-much per shelf? Such a person, if properly qualified, could make a fortune . . . How many uses of mauling would there be? Without giving the matter much thought, I should say four. Supposing an experienced handler is asked to quote for the handling of one shelf of books four feet in length. He would quote thus under four heads: –

'Popular handling – Each volume to be well and truly handled, four leaves in each to be dog-eared, and a tram ticket, cloak-room docket or other comparable article inserted in each as a forgotten book-mark. Say £1 7s 6d. Five per cent discount for civil servants.

Premier handling – Each volume to be thoroughly handled, eight leaves in each to be dog-eared, a suitable passage in not less than 25 volumes to be underlined in red pencil, and a leaflet in French on the works of Victor Hugo to be inserted as a forgotten book-mark in each. Say, £2 17s 6d. Five per cent discount for literary university students, civil servants and lady social workers.

. . .

De Luxe handling – Each volume to be mauled savagely, the spines of the smaller volumes to be damaged in a manner that will give the impression that they have been carried around in pockets, a passage in every volume to be underlined in red pencil with an exclamation point or interrogation mark inserted in the margin opposite, an Old Gate Theatre programme to be inserted in each volume as a forgotten book-mark . . . not less than 30 volumes to be treated with old coffee, tea, porter or whiskey stains, and not less than five volumes to be inscribed with the forged signature of the authors. Five per cent discount for bank managers, county surveyors and the heads of business houses employing not less than 35 hands. Dog-ears extra and inserted according to instructions, two pence per half dozen per volume. Quotations for alternative old Paris theatre programmes on demand. This service available for a limited time only, nett, £7 18s 3d.

. . .

Le traitment superbe – Every volume to be well and truly handled, first by a qualified handler and subsequently by a master-handler who shall have to his credit not less than 550 handling hours; suitable passages in not less than fifty per cent of the books to be underlined in good-quality red ink and an appropriate phrase from the following list in the margin, viz:

Rubbish!

Yes, indeed!

How true, how true!

I don't agree at all!

Why?

Yes, but cf. Homer, Od. iii, 151.

Well, well, well.

Quite, but Boussnet in his Discourse sur L'Histoire Universalle has already established the same point and given much more forceful explanations.

Nonsense! nonsense!

A point well taken!

But *why* in heaven's name!

I remember poor Joyce saying the very same thing to me.

Need I say that a special quotation may be obtained at any time for the supply of Special and Exclusive Phrases? The extra charge is not very much, really.'

Flann O'Brien, 'Buchhandlung' (1968).

*****

I am all for the giving and receiving of books at Christmas, though not keen either on giving or receiving 'gift books', the kind of tarted-up books which appear at this time of year and no other. I agree that the only thing you could do with such books is to give them away, and given away shall duly be any such as come into my possession without the formality of payment. Most of them are an awkward shape, anyhow – too tall or too wide or too small. They are encumbrances; I cannot afford them house room.

Daniel George, 'Gift books' (1947).

The unfinished or unread books languish on my shelves, some bought because friends said I must read them (but it was they who had to read them), or because the reviews throbbed with largesse of spirit (but it was the reviewer I loved, just as Priscilla loves John Alden, or Roxane Cyrano; I should have bought the reviewer's book). Others were just too gorgeously packaged to resist. Book jackets nowadays have become an art form, and browsing through a bookstore is a feast for the eyes. In some cases the jacket turns out to be the best thing about the book. I am not one to snub beauty, wherever it turns up. Yet I have come to distrust book jackets calculated to prick desire like a Bloomingdale's window, as if you could wear what you read. The great French novels used to come in plain shiny yellow jackets, and the drab Modern Library uniforms hid the most lavish loot.

Once in a while I take these castoffs down and turn their pages for exercise, stroke them a bit. They have the slightly dusty, forlorn patina of people seldom held or loved, while their neighbors stand upright with self-esteem, for having been known, partaken of intimacies. I am regretful, but my heart is hardened.

Lynne Sharon Schwartz, *Ruined by Reading* (1996).

If fortune made me possessor of one book of excessive value, I should hasten to part with it. In a little working library, to hold a first quarto of *Hamlet,* would be like entertaining a reigning monarch in a small farmhouse at harvesting.

Edmund Gosse, *Gossip in a Library* (1891).

✳ ✳ ✳ ✳ ✳

'I struck a fireman when he came to burn my library years ago. I've been running ever since. You want to join us, Montag?'
'Yes.'

'What have you to offer?'

'Nothing. I thought I had part of the Book of Ecclesiastes and maybe a little of Revelation, but I haven't even that now.'

'The Book of Ecclesiastes would be fine. Where was it?'

'Here,' Montag touched his head.

'Ah,' Granger smiled and nodded.

'What's wrong. Isn't that all right?' said Montag.

'Better than all right; perfect!' Granger turned to the Reverend. 'Do we have a Book of Ecclesiastes?'

'One. A man named Harris of Youngstown.'

'Montag.' Granger took Montag's shoulder firmly. 'Walk carefully. Guard your health. If anything should happen to Harris, *you* are the Book of Ecclesiastes. See how important you've become in the last minute!'

'But I've forgotten!'

'No, nothing's ever lost. We have ways to shake down your clinkers for you.'

'But I've tried to remember!'

'Don't try. It'll come when we need it. All of us have photographic memories, but spend a lifetime learning how to block off the things that are really *in* there. Simmons here has worked on it for twenty years and now we've got the method down to where we can recall anything that's been read once. Would you like, some day, Montag, to read Plato's *Republic*?'

'Of course!'

'*I* am Plato's *Republic*. Like to read Marcus Aurelius? Mr Simmons is Marcus.'

'How do you do?' said Mr Simmons.

'Hello,' said Montag.

'I want you to meet Jonathan Swift, the author of that evil political book *Gulliver's Travels*! And this other fellow is Charles Darwin, and this one is Schopenhauer, and this one is Einstein, and this one here at my elbow is Mr Albert Schweitzer, a very kind philosopher indeed. Here we all are,

Montag. Aristophanes and Mahatma Gandhi and Gautama Buddha and Confucius and Thomas Love Peacock and Thomas Jefferson and Mr Lincoln, if you please. We are also Matthew, Mark, Luke and John.'

Everyone laughed quietly.

'It can't *be*,' said Montag.

'It *is*,' replied Granger, smiling. '*We're* book-burners, too. We read the books and burn them, afraid they'd be found. Micro-filming didn't pay off; we were always travelling, we didn't want to bury the film and come back later. Always the chance of discovery. Better to keep it in the old heads, where no one can see it or suspect it. We are all bits and pieces of history and literature and international law, Byron, Tom Paine, Machiavelli, or Christ, it's here.'

Ray Bradbury, Fahrenheit 451 (1953).

✳ ✳ ✳ ✳ ✳

. . . whatever else it may be, a book is a manufactured item, which should be amusing to look at and pleasant to hold.

John Updike, 'A bookish boy'.

INDEX OF AUTHORS

SUBJECT INDEX

abomination, perpetrated by Cambridge
    tutor, 85
Amundsen, eating the sledge dogs, 136
annotation, a crime which should be
    denied benefit of clergy, 200
architecture of lift shafts, 170
arsenal, a perfect, 87
atlas, for mending window, 187
author
    books sent, 'best regards of', 198
    never despised by, 37
    signature forged, 201
authors
    arranged in neat pews, 83
    dream of passionate readers, 38
    like cattle, 83
    modern, dearth of in prison, 120
    pack let loose, 119
    revealing best thoughts, 39
    some ubiquitous, 110
autobiography, slip into pocket, 107

backs, gilded, 63
'Bad Bits', 200
barbarity, humanity lapsing back into,
    127
bargains, not to be had, 110
bath, reading in, 132
bathroom, colonies of prose formed in,
    88
baud, given her price, 106
be open to learn, 39
bears, something awful about, 198
bedroom, for novels and detective
    stories, 69
bee, troublesome, 52
best sellers, read as fast as possible, 83
Bible, smashing book for dog-ends, 182
bibliomania, ultimate excess, 64
bibliophagy, 60, 181
bibliophiles, abiding in the trenches, 199

bindings
    Cape goatskin, 175
    checked out, 191
    cowhide, 175
    handsome, 62
    new, 194
    not even subject to sunlight, 176
    productive of phthisis, 148
blasphemy, 23
blots, 197
blush, brought on by reading sociably, 84
bone, dog holding, 20
book
    a perfect gentleman in aspect and
      demeanour, 193
    amusing to look at, 205
    an innocent and becoming spectacle,
      191
    an instrument of tyranny, 168
    appropriate carrying important for
      peer acceptance, 77
    as friend, 121
    as murder weapon, 180
    as sloping desk, 178
    bad, not sacrosanct, 83
    battered, loathing of, 78
    been there mutely the whole time, 133
    bought for sake of its smell, 193
    burning, dead against, 161
    carrying is sexually dimorphic, 77
    centre of gravity, 75
    chosen with handbag-level care, 81
    corners eroded to board, 197
    corners, turning down, 172
    counting more than its independent
      value, 133
    determined to buy, 94
    difficult to tire of, 84
    disease, 83
    disguise adopted by Zeus, 185
    each lives a different life, 194

REFERENCES AND
COPYRIGHT NOTICES

Exhaustive efforts have been made to secure permissions, but the Editors may not always have succeeded in tracking the relevant copyright holder. We apologise for any omission: notification of such should be addressed to the Editors c/o the publisher.

Ackroyd, P. (1987) *Chatterton*, London: Hamish Hamilton. © Peter Ackroyd. Printed with permission of the author.

Aikin, J. (1795) *Letters from a Father to a Son*, Dublin: John Milliken.

Allen, W. (1983) *Four Films of Woody Allen*, London: Faber and Faber.

Arnold, Matthew (2001 [1882]) Matthew Arnold, letter to Frances Arnold, 1 January, 1882, in C. Y. Lang (ed.), *The Letters of Matthew Arnold, Vol. 5 1879–1884*, Charlottesville: University Press of Virginia.

Arnim, E. von (1990 [1904]) *The Adventures of Elizabeth in Rugen*, London: Virago Press.

Auden, W. H. (1963) 'Reading', in *The Dyer's Hand and Other Essays*, London: Faber and Faber.

Austen, J. (1972 [1813]) *Pride and Prejudice*, Harmondsworth: Penguin.

Auster, P. (1990) *Moon Palace*, London: Faber and Faber. © Paul Auster, 1989. Printed with permission of the author.

Bacon, F. (2002 [1625]) 'Of Studies', in B. Vickers (ed.), *Francis Bacon: A Critical Edition of the Major Works*, Oxford: Oxford University Press.

Baker, N. (1996 [1995]) 'Books as furniture', in *The Size of Thoughts: Essays and Other Lumber*, London: Chatto and Windus. © Nicholson Baker. Printed with permission of the author.

Barnes, J. (1984) *Flaubert's Parrot*, London: Jonathan Cape. © Julian Barnes. Printed by permission of PFD on behalf of Julian Barnes.

Battles, M. (2003) *Library: An Unquiet History*, London: William Heinemann. © Matthew Battles. Printed with permission of the author and publisher.

Beauvoir, S. de, trans. J. Kirkup (1959) *Memoirs of a Dutiful Daughter*, London: André Deutsch and Weidenfeld and Nicholson and 1963 Penguin Books © Librarie Gallimard, 1958. This translation © The World Publishing Company.

Beerbohm, M. (1911) *Zuleika Dobson*, London: William Heinemann and Dodd, Mead and Company.

Behan, B. (1980 [1958]) *Borstal Boy*, London: Corgi Books.

Bennett, Alan (2004) 'Austerity in colour', in *Guardian Review*, 7 February.

Bennett, Alan (1990) 'The treachery of books', in *Writing Home*, London: Faber and Faber (1994). © Forelake Ltd 1990. Reproduced by permission of PFD (www.pfd.co.uk) on behalf of Forelake Ltd.

Bennett, Arnold (1932 [1896]) 'Journal, 15 October, 1896', in N. Flower (ed.), *The Journals of Arnold Bennett 1896–1910*, London: Cassell and Company Ltd.

Bennett, Arnold (1902) *The Truth about an Author*, London: Constable and Co. Ltd.

Bennett, Arnold (1979 [1902]) 'Alone in London', in J. Hepburn (ed.), *Arnold Bennett, Sketches for an Autobiography*, London: George Allen and Unwin.

Bennett, Arnold (1946 [1907]) 'The death of Simon Fuge', in *The Grim Smile of the Five Towns*, Harmondsworth: Penguin.

Bennett, Arnold (1959 [1923]) *Riceyman Steps*, London: Cassell and Company.

Bennett, Arnold (1974[1928]) 'I read a "thriller" – and startle my friends', in A. Mylett, *Arnold Bennett: The Evening Standard Years 'Books and Persons' 1926–31*, London: Chatto and Windus.

Birkerts, S. (1987) 'Notes from a confession', in *An Artificial Wilderness*, New York: William Morrow and Company. © Sven Birkerts. Printed with permission of the author.

Birrell, A. (1905) 'Book buying' and 'Bookworms', in *In the Name of the Bodleian, and Other Essays*, London: Elliot Stock.

Blatchford, R. (1900) *My Favourite Books*, London: Clarion Press.

Blyton, E. (1964) *Birmingham Evening Mail*, 3 November, quoted in S. Ray (1982) *The Blyton Phenomenon: The Controversy Surrounding the World's Most Successful Children's Writer*, London: André Deutsch.

Boorstin, D. J. (1962) *The Image*, London: Weidenfeld and Nicholson.

Boswell, J. (1969 [1791]) *Life of Johnson*, London: Oxford University Press.

Boyd, W. (1987) *The New Confessions*, London: Hamish Hamilton. © William Boyd. Printed with permission of the author.

Bradbury, R. (1976 [1953]) *Fahrenheit 451*, London: Flamingo.

Brenan, G. (1962) *A Life of One's Own*, London: Hamish Hamilton. All rights reserved. Extract reproduced with permission of the Estate of Gerald Brenan c/o Margaret Hanbury, 27 Walcot Square, London, SE11 4UB.

Brodkey, H. (1985) 'Reading: the most dangerous game', in *The New York Times Book Review*, November 11.

Brontë, C. (1977 [1847]) *Jane Eyre*, Harmondsworth: Penguin.

Brown, J. (1907 [1861]) 'Letter to John Cairns, D.D.' and 'With brains, Sir!', in *Horae Subsecivae*, London: Oxford University Press.

Browne, M. (1866) 'On the forming of opinions on books', in *Views and Opinions*, London: Alexander Strahan.

Browning, E. B. (1882 [1856]) *Aurora Leigh*, London: Smith, Elder and Co.

Browning, G. (2003) 'How to . . . read', in *The Guardian Weekend Magazine*, 5 April. © Guy Browning. Printed with permission of the author.

Bukowski, C. (2000 [1982]) *Ham on Rye*, Edinburgh: Canongate.

Burton, J. H. (1862) *The Book-Hunter*, Edinburgh: William Blackwood and Sons.

Bury, R. de (1929 [1599]) *Philobiblon*, extract in F. H. Pritchard (ed.), *Great Essays of All Nations*, London: George C. Harrap and Co.

Butler, F. and Hartman, F. (1942) *The Road to Morocco*, Paramount Pictures.

Butler, S. (1979 [*c*.1660s]) 'Prose Observations', in H. de Quehen (ed.), *Samuel Butler, Prose Observations*, Oxford: Clarendon Press.

Butler, S. (1968 [1888]) 'Ramblings in Cheapside' and 'Quis desiderio', in *Collected Essays Volume II*, New York: AMS Press.

Calvino, I. (1979) *If on a Winter's Night a Traveller*, London: Vintage.

Canetti, E., trans. C. V. Wedgwood (1965 [1935]) *Auto da Fé*, Harmondsworth, Penguin. Reprinted by permission of The Random House Group Ltd.

Canetti, E. (1987 [1979]) *Conscience of Words and Earwitness*, London: Picador.

Canetti, E. (1978 [1943]) *The Human Province*, New York: Seabury Press.

Carlyle, T. (1891 [1843]) 'On a proper choice of reading', in R. Cochrane (ed.), *The English Essayists: A Comprehensive Selection from the Words of the Great Essayists*, Edinburgh: W. P. Nimmo, Hay and Mitchell.

Carroll, L. (1965 [1865]) *Alice in Wonderland*, Harmondsworth: Penguin.

Chambers, W. (1872) *Memoir of Robert Chambers: with Autobiographic Reminiscences of William Chambers*, Edinburgh: W. & R. Chambers.

Chaucer, G., trans. N. Coghill (1960 [*c*.1380s] *The Canterbury Tales*, Harmondsworth: Penguin.

Chaucer, G., trans. B. Stone (1983 [*c*.1385–6]) *The Legend of Good Women*, Harmondsworth: Penguin.

Chesterfield, Lord (1929 [1774]) *Letters to his Son and Others*, London: J. M. Dent & Sons Ltd.

Christie, M. E. (1898) 'Recollections of my grandfather's library', in *Mock Essays and Character Sketches*, London: William Rice.

Cobbett, W. (1947 [1855]) *Autobiography*, London: Faber and Faber.

Colby, F. M. (1926) 'The books I haven't read', in *The Colby Essays*, vol. II, New York: Harper and Brothers.

Colton, C. C. (1820) *Lacon: Or Many Things in Few Words; Addressed to Those Who Think*, London: Longman, Hurst, Rees Orme and Brown.

Connolly, C. (1961 [1938]) 'Reviewers', in *Enemies of Promise*, Harmondsworth: Penguin. © Cyril Connolly. Reproduced by permission of the author c/o Rogers, Coleridge & White Ltd., 20 Powis Mews, London W11 1JN.

Connolly, C. (1945) 'The novel-addict's cupboard', in *The Condemned Playground. Essays: 1927–1944*, London: Routledge. Originally published by Hogarth Press. Reprinted by permission of The Random House Group Ltd.

Conrad, J. (1925 [1905]) 'Books', in *Notes on Life and Letters*, Edinburgh: John Grant.

Crothers, S. M. (1906) *The Gentle Reader*, Boston: Houghton, Mifflin and Co.

Cuppy, W. (1950) *The Decline and Fall of Practically Everybody*, New York: Holt.

Dante, trans. H. F. Carey (1908 [*c*.1307]) *The Divine Comedy of Dante*, London: J. M. Dent and Sons Ltd.

Davenport, G. (1990 [1987]) 'On reading', in D. Halpern (ed.) *Antæus: Literature as Pleasure*, London: Collins Harvill. Printed with permission.

Davies, R. (1990) 'Reading', in *Reading and Writing*, Salt Lake City: University of Utah Press.

Davies, R. (1980 [1951]) *Tempest-Tost*, published within *The Salterton Trilogy*, Harmondsworth: Penguin.

Descartes, R., trans. F. E. Sutcliffe, (1958 [1637]) *Discourse on Method*, Harmondsworth: Penguin

Dickens, C. (1984 [1843–4]) *Martin Chuzzlewit*, Harmondsworth: Penguin.

Dickens, C. (1994 [1837–9]) *Oliver Twist*, Harmondsworth: Penguin.

Dobson, A. (1917) *A Bookman's Budget*, London: Oxford University Press.

Driffield, B. C. M. (1985) *Driff's Guide to All the Secondhand Bookshops in Britain*, London: BCM Driffield.

Eco, U. (1983) *The Name of the Rose*, London: Secker and Warburg. © Gruppo Editoriale Fabbri-Bompiani, Sonzogno, Etas S.p.A., English translation by W. Weaver © 1983 by Harcourt, Inc. and Martin Secker & Warburg Limited. Reprinted by permission of Harcourt, Inc.

Eliot, G. (1913 [1876]) *Daniel Deronda*, Edinburgh: William Blackwood and Sons.

Eliot, G. (1913 [1858]), 'Janet's Repentence', from *Scenes from Clerical Life*, Edinburgh: William Blackwood and Sons.

Emerson, R. W. (1903 [1860]) 'Books', in *The Complete Prose Works of Ralph Waldo Emerson*, London: Ward, Lock and Co Ltd.

Epstein, J. (1985) 'The noblest distraction', in *Plausible Prejudices*, New York: W. W. Norton. © Joseph Epstein. Printed with permission of the author.

Erasmus, D. *Colloquies: Of the Method of Study; To Christianus of Lubeck*, quoted in A. Ireland (1883) *The Book-Lover's Enchiridion*, London: Simkind, Marshall and Co.

Fadiman, A. (2000 [1998]) *Ex Libris: Confessions of a Common Reader*, Harmondsworth: Penguin.

Fischer, T. (2001) 'Bookcruncher', in *Don't Read This Book if You're Stupid*, London: Vintage. © Tibor Fischer. Printed with permission of the author.

Fitzgerald, F. S. (1991 [1925]) *The Great Gatsby*, London: Everyman. Printed with permission.

Fitzgerald, F. S. (1968 [1940]) Fitzgerald, F. S., letter to Zelda, 4 May, 1940, in A. Turnbull (ed.), *The Letters of F. Scott Fitzgerald*, Harmondsworth: Penguin. Printed with permission.

Fitzgerald, P. (1997 [1978]) *The Bookshop*, Boston: Houghton Mifflin. © 1978 by Penelope Fitzgerald. Reprinted by permission of Houghton Mifflin Company and HarperCollins Publishers Ltd. All rights reserved.

Fletcher, J. (1624/5) *The Elder Brother*, in (1994) *The Dramatic Works in the Beaumont and Fletcher Canon*, vol. IX, Cambridge: Cambridge University Press.

Foot, M. (1980) 'Isaac Foot: A Rupert for the Roundheads', in *Debts of Honour*, London: Picador.

Fowles, J. (1975) 'Of memoirs and magpies', *Atlantic Monthly*, June. © John Fowles. Printed with permission.

Frazier, C. (1998 [1997]) *Cold Mountain*, Polmont: Sceptre. Reprinted by permission of International Creative Management Inc. Copyright ©1997.

Fuller, T. (1892 [1662]) *The History of the Worthies of England*, in A. Jessopp (ed.), *Wide Words and Quaint Counsels of Thomas Fuller*, Oxford, Clarendon Press.

Gallienne, R. Le (1896) *Retrospective Reviews: A Literary Log*, London: John Lane.

Gardam, J. (1992) quoted in A. Fraser (ed.), *The Pleasure of Reading*, London: Bloomsbury. © Antonia Fraser. Permission granted by Curtis Brown Group Ltd.

Gaskell, E. (1996 [1863]) *Sylvia's Lovers*, Harmondsworth: Penguin.

George, D. (1954) 'Gift books' and 'The reading habit', in *Lonely Pleasures*, London: Jonathan Cape.

Gibbon, E. (1972 [1796]) *Autobiography of Edward Gibbon*, Lord Sheffield (ed.), Oxford: Oxford University Press.

Gide, A., trans. D. Bussy (1951 [1920]) *If it Die*, London: Secker and Warburg. Reprinted by permission of The Random House Group Ltd.

Gilchrist, E. (1991 [1981]) 'Indignities', in *In the Land of Dreamy Dreams*, London: Faber and Faber.

Gissing, G. (1961 [1903]) *The Private Papers of Henry Ryecroft*, Brighton: Harvester Books.

Gorky, M., trans. R. Wilks (1983 [1915]) *My Apprenticeship*, Harmondsworth: Penguin. © Ronald Wilks, 1974. Reproduced by permission of Penguin Books Ltd.

Gosse, E. (1891) *Gossip in a Library*, London: William Heinemann.

Grahame, K. (1894) 'Non libri sed liberi', in *Pagan Papers*, London: Elkin Matthews and John Lane.

Greene, G. (1966 [1951] 'Book market', in *The Lost Childhood and Other Essays*, Harmondsworth: Penguin. Reprinted with permission.

Greene, G. (1978) *The Human Factor*, Harmondsworth: Penguin. Reprinted with permission.

Greer, G. (1990) *Daddy, We Hardly Knew You*, United States: Random House.

Greer, G. (1992) quoted in Antonia Fraser (ed.), *The Pleasure of Reading*, London: Bloomsbury.

Grey, Viscount (1924) 'The pleasure of reading', in *The Fallodon Papers*, London: Constable and Co. Ltd.

Grigson, G. (1980) 'For liquid flies', in *History of Him*, London: Secker and Warburg. Reproduced with permission.

Guardian, The (2004) 'I like to read', 29 May.

Hanaway, T. and G. Burghardt (1976) 'The development of sexually dimorphic book-carrying behaviour', *Journal of the Psychonomic Society*, 7, 3, pp. 267–70. Printed with permission of the authors.

Hanff, H. (1984 [1971]) *84, Charing Cross Road*, London: Futura.

Hare, A. W. & J. C. (1897 [1827]) *Guesses at Truth*, in P. E. G. Girdlestone, *Guesses at Truth: Selections from the work of Augustus and Julius Hare*, London: George Routledge and Sons.

Hayakawa, S. I. (1952) *Language in Thought and Action*, London: George Allen and Unwin Ltd.

Hazlitt, W. (n.d. [1817]) 'On reading old books', in *Essays and Characters*, London: Thomas Nelson and Sons Ltd.

Hazlitt, W. (1902 [1839]) 'On reading new books', in *Sketches and Essays*, London: Grant Richards.

Hoban, R. (1975) *Turtle Diary*, London: Jonathan Cape Ltd. © Russell Hoban. Reprinted with permission of the author.

Holmes, O. W. (1888) *The Breakfast Table Series*, London: George Routledge and Sons.

Holroyd, M. (1971) *Lytton Strachey: A Biography*, Harmondsworth: Penguin. © Michael Holroyd. Printed with permission of the author.

Howe, E. W. (1911) *Country Town Sayings: A Collection of Paragraphs from the Atchison Globe by E. W. Howe*, Topeka, Kansas: Cromer and Company.

Hughes, R. (1996) quoted in A. Jones, S. Smith and M. Thomson (eds), *Chambers Dictionary of Quotations*, Edinburgh: Chambers Harrap Publishers Ltd.

Hunt, L. (1911 [c.1820]) *Retrospective Review*, quoted in R. M. Leonard (ed.), *The Book Lover's Anthology*, London: Oxford University Press.)

Hunt, L. (1916 [1823]) 'My books', in R. B. Johnson (ed.), *Essays and Sketches by Leigh Hunt*, London: Oxford University Press.

Hunt, L. (1883 [1837]) 'Old books and bookshops: the beneficence of book-stalls', quoted in A. Ireland (ed.), *The Book-Lover's Enchiridion*, London: Simkin, Marshall and Co.

Huxley, A. (2000 [1925]) 'Books for the journey', in R. Baker and J. Sexton (eds), *Aldous Huxley Complete Essays Volume I, 1920–25*. Chicago: Ivan R. Dee. Reprinted with permission.

Huxley, A. (2001 [1936]) 'Writers and readers', in R. Baker and J. Sexton (eds) *Aldous Huxley Complete Essays Volume IV, 1936–8*. Chicago: Ivan R. Dee. Reprinted with permission.

Huysmans, J.-K., trans. J. Howard [1922 (1884)] *Against the Grain*, New York: Lieber and Lewis.

Irving, J. (1983 [1976]) *The World According to Garp*, London: Corgi. © John Irving. Printed with permission of the author.

Irving, W. (1996 [1820–1]) 'The art of book-making' and 'The mutability of literature', in *The Sketch-Book of Geoffrey Crayon, Gent*, Oxford: Oxford University Press.

Ishiguro, K. (1989) *The Remains of the Day*, London: Faber and Faber.

James, H. (1981 [1888]) 'London', in *English Hours*, Oxford: Oxford University Press.

James, H. (1976 [1881]) *The Portrait of a Lady*, Harmondsworth: Penguin.

Jerrold, D. (1894) *Mrs Caudle's Curtain Lectures*, London: George Routledge and Sons Ltd.

Keats, J. (1935 [1819]) John Keats, letter to Fanny Keats, 28 August, 1819, in M. B. Forman, *The Letters of John Keats*, London: Oxford University Press.

Keillor, G. (1991) *Radio Romance*, London: Faber and Faber. Reprinted with permission.

Kingsley, H. (1883 [1862]) *Ravenshoe*, London: Ward, Lock and Co Ltd.

Kipling, R. (1937) *Something of Myself*, London: Macmillan and Co.

Lamb, C. (1976 [1802]) Charles Lamb, letter to Samuel Taylor Coleridge, 11 October, 1802, in E. W. Marrs, *The Letters of Charles and Mary Anne Lamb*, Cornell University Press: Ithaca.

Lamb, C. (1903 [1833]) 'Detached thoughts on books and reading', in *The Last Essays of Elia*, in E. V. Lucas (ed.), *The Works of Charles and Mary Lamb*, vol. II, London: Methuen and Co.

Lang, A. (1913) *Books and Bookmen*, London: Longman's Green and Co.

Larkin, P. (1983 [1972]) 'Books', reprinted in *Required Writing, Miscellaneous Pieces 1955–1982*, London: Faber and Faber.

Laski, H. (1953[1925/26]) Howard Laski, letter to Justice Holmes, 13 June, 1925 and 26 August, 1926, in M. De Wolfe Howe, *Holmes-Laski Letters: The Correspondence of Mr Justice Holmes and Harold J. Laski*, London: Geoffrey Cumerlege.

Lennox, C. (1989 [1752]) *The Female Quixote*, Oxford: Oxford University Press.

Lewis, S. (1950 [1920]) *Main Street: The Story of Carol Kennicott*, United States: Harcourt, Brace and World, Inc. ©1920 by Harcourt, Inc. and renewed 1948 by Sinclair Lewis. Reprinted by permission of the publisher.

Long, D. (1990 [1987]) 'On rereading', in D. Halpern (ed.), *Antaeus: Literature as Pleasure*, London: Collins Harvill. Reprinted by permission of The Random House Group Ltd.

Lowe, R. (1911 [1869]) 'Speech to the students of the Croydon Science and Art Schools', quoted in R. M. Leonard (ed.), *The Book-Lover's Anthology*, London: Oxford University Press.

Lucas, E. V. (1907) 'A funeral', in *Character and Comedy*, London: Methuen and Company.

Lynd, R. (1923) 'Out of print', in *The Blue Lion and Other Essays*, London: Methuen and Co. Ltd.

Macaulay, R. (1925) *A Casual Commentary*, London: Methuen and Co.

Macaulay, R. (1989 [1941]) 'Losing one's books', in F. Glass and P. Marsden-Smedley (eds), *Articles of War: The Spectator Book of World War II*, London: Grafton Books. © The Spectator.

Manguel, A. (1996) *A History of Reading*, London: HarperCollins. © Alberto Manguel. Printed with permission of the author.

Mansfield, K. (1928 [1922]) Katherine Mansfield, letter to Lady Ottoline Morrell, January 1922, in J. M. Murray, *The Letters of Katherine Mansfield, Vol. II*, London: Constable and Co. Ltd.

Maugham, W. S. (1951) 'The book bag', in *The Complete Short Stories,* vol. III, London: Vintage. Reprinted by permission of The Random House Group Ltd.

Maugham, W. S. (1944) *The Razor's Edge*, London: Heinemann. Reprinted by permission of The Random House Group Ltd.

Mayhew, H. (1965 [1861–2]) 'Of the character of books of the street-sale', in *Selections from London Labour and the London Poor*, London: Oxford University Press.

McMurtry, L. (1999) *Walter Benjamin at the Dairy Queen*, New York: Simon Schuster. © Larry McMurtry. Reprinted with permission of the author.

Mehta, G. (1992) quoted in A. Fraser (ed.) *The Pleasure of Reading*, London: Bloomsbury. © Antonia Fraser. Permission granted by Curtis Brown Group Ltd.

Michaels, A. (1998 [1997]) *Fugitive Pieces*, London: Boomsbury. © Anne Michaels. Reprinted with permission of the author.

Miller, H. (1969) 'They were alive and they spoke to me' and 'Letter to Pierre Lesdain', in *The Books in My Life*, New York: New Directions. © New Directions Publishing Corp. Reprinted by permission of New Directions Publishing Corp.

Milton, J. (1980 [1671]) *Paradise Regained*, in *The Complete English Poems*, London: Everyman's Library.

Mitford, N. (2003 [1945]) *The Pursuit of Love*, London: Penguin.

Montaigne, M. de, trans. C. Cotton (1883 [1580]) 'Of three commerces', in A. Ireland (ed.), *The Book-Lover's Enchiridion*, London: Simkin, Marshall and Co.

Morley, C. (1925) 'On visiting bookshops', in *Safety Pins and Other Essays*, London: Jonathan Cape.

Morley, E. J. (ed.) *Henry Crabb Robinson on Books and their Writers*, vol. I, London: J. M. Dent and Sons.

Morell, A. (1995) *A Camera in a Room, Photographs by Aberlardo Morell*, C. Sullivan (ed.), Washington: Smithsonian Institute Press

Munby, A. N. L. (1952) 'Floreat bibliomania', in *Essays and Papers*, London: The Scholar Press. Printed with permission.

Mylett, A. (1974) *Arnold Bennett: The Evening Standard Years 'Books and Persons' 1926–31*, London: Chatto and Windus.

Naipaul, V. S. (2001 [1957]) *The Mystic Masseur*, London: Picador. © V. S. Naipaul. Reprinted with permission.

Nicholson, H. (1937) 'How to read books', in *Small Talk*, London: Constable and Co. Ltd.

Norwood, G. (1926) 'Too many books', in *The Wooden Man and Other Stories and Essays*, London: William Heinemann Ltd.

O'Brien, F. (1968) 'Buchhandlung', in *The Best of Myles*, London: MacGibbon and Kee. © The Estate of the Late Brian O'Nolan. Reproduced by permission of A. M. Heath & Company Ltd. on behalf of the Estate.

O'Brien, F. (1990) 'The forgetting of eaten bread', in *Myles Away from Dublin*, London: Paladin Grafton Books. © The Estate of the Late Brian O'Nolan. Reproduced by permission of A. M. Heath & Company Ltd. on behalf of the Estate.

O'Casey, S. (1980 [1939]) *I Knock at the Door*, London: Pan Classics.

Ondaatje, M. (1992) *The English Patient*, London: Bloomsbury.

Orwell, G. (1984 [1936]) 'Bookshop memories', in *The Penguin Essays of George Orwell*, Harmondsworth: Penguin. © George Orwell. Permission granted by Bill Hamilton as the Literary Executor of the Estate of the Late Sonia Brownell Orwell and Martin Secker & Warburg Ltd.

Orwell, G. (1939) *Coming up for Air*, London: Victor Gollancz. © George Orwell. Permission granted by Bill Hamilton as the Literary Executor of the Estate of the Late Sonia Brownell Orwell and Martin Secker & Warburg Ltd. For the US, reprint by permission of Harcourt, Inc.

Orwell, G. (1946) 'Confessions of a book reviewer', in P. Davidson (ed.), *The Complete Works of George Orwell, Volume 18: Smothered Under Journalism 1946,* London: Secker and Warburg. © George Orwell. Permission granted by Bill Hamilton as the Literary Executor of the Estate of the Late Sonia Brownell Orwell and Martin Secker & Warburg Ltd.

Palmer, S. (1974 [1880]) Samuel Palmer, letter to Charles West Cape, 31 January, 1880, in R. Lister (ed.), *The Letters of Samuel Palmer, Vol. II,* Oxford: Clarendon Press.

Pater, W. (1985 [1885]) *Marius the Epicurean,* Harmondsworth: Penguin.

Peacock, T. L. (1893 [1831]) *Crotchet Castle,* London: J. M. Dent and Co.

Peake, M. (1976 [1946]) *Titus Groan,* Harmondsworth: Penguin. Reprinted with permission.

Pérez-Reverte, A. (2003 [1993]) *The Dumas Club,* London: Vintage.

Peter, J. (1989) reviewing Ian Charleson's *Hamlet, The Sunday Times,* 12 November.

Potter, S. (1952) 'Litmanship', in *The Complete One Upmanship,* London: Granada Publishing.

Powys, J. C. (1974 [1929]) *The Meaning of Culture,* London: Village Press. Reproduced by Pollinger Limited and the proprietor.

Pratchett, T. (1989) *Guards! Guards!,* London: Victor Gollancz Ltd.

Pratchett, T. and S. Briggs (1994) *The Discworld Companion,* London: Victor Gollancz.

Proust, M., trans. J. Sturrock (1998 [1905]) 'Days of Reading I', in *Against Sainte-Beuve and Other Essays,* Harmondsworth: Penguin.

Quincey, T. de (1970 [1839]) 'William Wordsworth and Robert Southey', in *Recollections of the Lakes and the Lake Poets,* Harmondsworth: Penguin.

Raban, J. (1987) *For Love and Money,* London: Collins Harvill. © Jonathan Raban. Printed with permission of the author.

Ransome, A. (1929) 'On reading too fast', in *Manchester Guardian.*

Rhys, J. (1981) *Smile Please: An Unfinished Autobiography,* Harmondsworth: Penguin. © Jean Rhys. Reproduced by permission of Sheil Land Associates Ltd on behalf of Jean Rhys Ltd.

Richardson, C. F. (1881) *The Choice of Books,* London: Sampson, Low, Marston, Searle and Rivington.

Rousseau, J.-J. (1904 [1781]) *The Confessions of Jean-Jacques Rousseau, Vol. I,* Edinburgh: Oliver and Boyd.

Ruskin, J. (1893 [1864]) *Sesame and Lilies,* London: George Allen.

Russell, B. (1978 [1967]) *Autobiography,* London: Unwin Paperbacks.

Russell, B. (1930) *The Conquest of Happiness,* Woking: Unwin Brothers.

Russell, G. W. E. (1914) 'Books', in *Selected Essays on Literary Subjects,* London: Dent and Sons.

Sage, L. (2000) *Bad Blood,* London: 4th Estate. Reprinted with permission.

Sartre, J.-P., trans. I. Clephane (1979 [1964]) *Words,* Harmondsworth: Penguin. *Les Mots* first published in France 1964, and by Penguin Books in 1967. Copyright © Editions Gallimard, 1964. Translation © Hamish Hamilton Ltd, 1964.

Schlink, B. (1998 [1997]) *The Reader,* London: Phoenix. © B. Schlink. Printed with permission of the author.

Schopenhauer, A. (1891[1851]) 'On reading and books' and 'On books and writing', in E. Belford, *Selected Essays of Arthur Schopenhauer with a Bibliographical Introduction of Sketch of His Philosophy*, London: George Bell and Sons.

Schwartz, L. S. (1996) *Ruined by Reading*, Boston: Beacon Press. © Lynne Sharon Schwartz. Printed with permission of the author.

Scott, W. (1894 [1814]) *Waverley*, London: Adam and Charles Black.

Seldon, J. (1890 [1689]) in S. W. Singer (ed.), *The Table-Talk of John Selden*, London: Reeves and Turner.

Self, W. (2002 [1999]) *Granta 65*, Spring 1999 in *Feeding Frenzy*, Harmondsworth: Penguin. © Will Self. Printed with permission of the author.

Seth, V. (1994 [1993]) *A Suitable Boy*, London: Phoenix House.

Shakespeare, W. (1990 [1594]) *Titus Andronicus* and *Love's Labour's Lost* in *The Complete Works of William Shakespeare*, London: Collins.

Sheffield, Lord (ed.) (1972 [1796]) *The Autobiography of Edward Gibbon*, Oxford: Oxford University Press.

Shenstone, W. (1891 [1769]) 'On writing and books', quoted in R. Cochrane (ed.), *The English Essayists: A Comprehensive Selection from the Works of the Great Essayists*, Edinburgh: W. P. Nimmo, Hay and Mitchell.

Simpson, A. and R. Galton (1960) *Hancock's Half Hour: The Missing Page*, available on BBC video, catalogue BBCV4037.

Škvorecký, J. (1990 [1987]) 'The pleasures of the freedom to read', in D. Halpern (ed.), *Antaeus: Literature as Pleasure*, London: Collins Harvill. © Joseph Škvorecký. Printed with permission of the author.

Slater, N. (2003) *Toast: The Story of a Boy's Hunger*, London: 4th Estate.

Smith, S. (1934 [1875]) in H. Pearson, *The Smith of Smith: Being the Life, Wit and Humour of Sydney Smith*, London: Hamish Hamilton.

Spender, S. (1989) *The Independent Magazine*, 18 November.

Spufford, F. (2002) *The Child that Books Built*, London: Faber and Faber. © 2002 by Francis Spufford. Reprinted by permission of Henry Holt and Company.

Squire, J. C. (1927) 'On destroying boks, 'Reading in bed' and 'Moving a library', in *Life at the Mermaid and Other Essays*, London: Kingsway Classics.

Steinbeck, J. (1954) quoted in R. T. Tripp (1973) *The International Thesaurus of Quotations*, London: George Allen and Unwin.

Stevenson, R. L. (1900 [1881]) *Virginibus Puerisque: and Other Papers*, London: Chatto and Windus.

Taylor, A., *The List*, 22–29 August (1988).

Tennyson, A. H. (1897) *Alfred Lord Tennyson: A Memoir by His Son*, vol. II, London: Macmillan and Co.

Tomlinson, H. M. (1918) 'Bed-books and night-lights', in *Old Junk*, London: Andrew Melrose.

Trelawny, E. (1905 [1878]) *Records of Shelley, Byron and the Author*, London: George Routledge and Sons, Ltd.

Trevelyan, G. (1876) *The Life and Letters of Lord Macaulay*, London: Longmans, Green and Co.

Trollope, A. (1991 [1855]) *The Warden*, London: Everyman's Library.

Trollope, A. (1974 [1883]) *An Autobiography*, London: Oxford University Press.

Twain, M. (1988) in A. Ayres (ed.), *Greatly Exaggerated: Wit and Wisdom of Mark Twain*, London: Barrie and Jenkins.

Updike, J. (1992) *Odd Jobs: Essays and Criticism*, London: André Deutsch.

Walpole, H. (1926) *These Diversions: Reading*, London: Jarrolds.

Waugh, E., edited and with notes by R. M. Davis (2003 [1934]) *A Handful of Dust*, London: Penguin. Also Chapman and Hall (1934) and Penguin Classics (2000). © Evelyn Waugh, 1930. © Introduction and notes, Robert Murray Davis.

Waugh, E. (1943 [1939]) 'An Englishman's home', in *Work Suspended and Other Stories*, London: Chapman and Hall. Also Chapman and Hall (1948) and Penguin Books (1951, 1982, 2000, 2000). © Evelyn Waugh, 1948.

Waugh, E. (1930) *Vile Bodies,* London: Chapman and Hall. Also Penguin Books (1938, 1996, 2000, 2003). © Evelyn Waugh, 1930, 1958. For the US: by permission of Little, Brown and Co. Inc.

Wharton, E. (1991 [1905]) *The House of Mirth*, London: Everyman's Library.

Wharton, E. (1993 [1920]) *The Age of Innocence,* London: Everyman. Reprinted by permission of the Estate of Edith Wharton and the Watkins/Loomis Agency.

Wharton, E. (1934) *A Backward Glance*, United States: Appleton Century. Reprinted by permission of the Estate of Edith Wharton and the Watkins/Loomis Agency.

Whitaker, B. (1992) *Notes & Queries*, vol. 3, London: Fourth Edition. © Guardian Newspapers Limited 1992.

Whitman, G. (2004) 'A life in the day', *Sunday Times Magazine*, 25 January. Printed with permission of the author.

Woolf, V. (1992 [1919]) *Night and Day,* London: Penguin. Reprinted with permission of The Society of Authors as the Literary Representative of the Estate of Virginia Woolf.

Wyndham, J. (1986) *Love is Blue: A Wartime Diary*, London: Heinemann. © Joan Wyndham. Printed with permission of the author.

Zacharias, L. (1990 [1987]) 'In the Garden of the Word', in D. Halpern (ed.), *Antaeus: Literature as Pleasure*, London: Collins Harvill. © Lee Zacharias. Printed with permission of the author.